CW00816295

MAN
YOUR
SOLVENCY

MANAGING
YOUR
SOLVENCY

A guide to insolvency and how to
ensure that you continue as a
going concern

edited by
Michael Norton

A DIRECTORY OF SOCIAL CHANGE PUBLICATION

MANAGING YOUR SOLVENCY
A guide to insolvency and how to ensure that you
continue as a going concern.

Edited by Michael Norton

Copyright © 1994 Directory of Social Change

First published 1994 by
Directory of Social Change
Radius Works, Back Lane, London NW3 1HL
from whom copies can be obtained.

Directory of Social Change is registered charity no. 800517

ISBN 1 873860 28 5

British Library Cataloguing in Publication Data
A catalogue record for this book is available from the
British Library.

Designed and typeset by Diarmuid Burke
Printed and bound by Page Brothers, Norwich

CONTENTS

FOREWORD

This is a book about the dangers and problems of **insolvency** and how to avoid it. But it is also a book about **solvency**. In the present funding climate for charities and other voluntary organisations, and with increased emphasis that many voluntary organisations are placing on earning their money from contracts and through marketing their services, it is as important for such organisations to create a robust financial structure for their operations that will enable them to come through periods of difficulty – and remain solvent – as it is for those organisations operating at the margin to prevent themselves from tumbling into the abyss.

The concern with solvency and insolvency is also a consequence of the 1993 Charities Act. This introduces new accounting standards for charities (due to come into force in 1994), which will focus attention on liabilities and contingent liabilities – and whether the charity has sufficient assets to cover these. The Act also emphasises the personal responsibility that charity trustees have to see that the affairs of their charity are in good order, and to ensure not only that the charity is meeting the needs of its beneficiaries, but that it will be there in future to meet the needs of future beneficiaries.

The book is aimed at

- **Charity Trustees** – all the trustees – as they have collective responsibility for the affairs of the charity, and at the members of the management committees of non-charitable voluntary organisations. But particularly at the Chair and the Treasurer who have more specific reasons for being concerned

- **Charity and Voluntary Organisation Directors** and **Financial Directors**, and throughout the book there are very practical ideas which might be relevant, and which could be put to the trustees for decision

- **Professional Advisers**, especially accountants and auditors. Charity and voluntary sector finances are, in some respects, very different from the finances of commercial concerns, and some of the issues and ideas discussed in this book may not be universally familiar in the professional accountancy world

- **Advisers**, including intermediary organisations and consultants, responsible for advising on management and financial strategies

- **Funders**, and especially local authorities, other statutory funders and grantmaking trusts. Many funders are concerned to see that the organisations they want to support are well enough funded and structurally sound enough to do a good job. Often the funders have been part of the problem – by underfunding (partly as a result of grant-seekers applying for too little in the first place, because they think that paring down an application will increase its chances of success), or through clawback (if a grant is not fully spent or funds are raised elsewhere). This has created an often under-resourced voluntary sector, just at the time when there are great changes and challenges. This book gives the funder a chance to be part of the solution.

The book has been produced collectively by a group of people with different perspectives on the problem. Its genesis was a discussion at the Charity Law Conference in January 1993, where it was apparent that issues of solvency and viability were of wide concern. A small working group was convened to discuss what might be done, and this book is the result.

The team who have contributed to the book include lawyers and accountants specialising in charities, an insolvency practitioner, and 'experts' with financial and management expertise. The book consists of a series of contributions offering a range of perspectives on the meaning and implications of insolvency and the importance of maintaining a robust organisation which is able to continue as a going concern. Inevitably there is some overlap between the different chapters. Some of this overlap has been edited out, but some has been retained to allow each contributor to make the points that they felt to be important from their own particular perspective on the problem.

We hope that the book will fulfil a valuable role in highlighting an area of interest and concern to charities and their supporters, and by presenting a number of practical steps which might be taken to improve the robustness and the long-term financial health of charities and other voluntary organisations.

About the contributors

Stephen Lloyd is a partner with solicitors Bates Wells and Braithwaite, an expert in charity law, a frequent speaker at seminars and conferences, and author of a publication on *Charity Trading and Charity Law*.

Peter Gotham is a partner in Gotham & Co, Chartered Accountants, who specialise in the not-for-profit and small business sectors. He is also a partner in Taylor Gotham, Insolvency Practitioners, and is a Licensed Insolvency Practitioner with (unfortunately) considerable experience in charity insolvency.

Adrian Randall is Director of Finance of the Cancer Research Campaign. He is also Professor of Accounting at South Bank University, Chairman of the Charities' Tax Reform Group and a co-founder and the first Chairman of the Charity Finance Directors Group.

Pesh Framjee is the partner in charge of the Charity Unit at BDO Binder Hamlyn Chartered Accountants which acts for over 350 charities. He is also co-ordinator of the Charity Finance Directors Group and writes and lectures extensively.

Lindsay Driscoll is Legal Adviser to the National Council for Voluntary Organisations, spending most of her working life dispensing advice and speaking at conferences.

R Greyham Dawes is an accountant on the staff of the Charity Commission, which has concerns for the financial health of charities as well as to support the role of trustees in their governance and supervision.

Kate Sayer is a partner in Sayer Vincent, a firm of accountants specialising in charity, housing association and voluntary sector accounts. She is a co-organiser of the annual Charity Accountants Conference, and she and her staff do extensive training on accounting and financial management for charities and voluntary organisations.

Michael Norton is Director of the Directory of Social Change, a national charity promoting effective management and good practice in the voluntary sector, which runs an extensive nation-wide programme of technical training for charities. He is co-author of *Accounting and Financial Management for Charities*.

The editor would also like to thank:

Sandy Adirondack, an independent trainer and consultant and author of *Just About Managing*, for a thorough reading of the manuscript and helpful comments to the text.

Mike Hudson, a partner in Compass Partnership for his help with Chapter 7.

This book is a distillation of the technical expertise, experience, ideas and wisdom of these ten people who together comprised the Insolvency Working Group.

Terms used

Charities come in a variety of different legal structures. The titles of those responsible for their governance and their legal duties and responsibilities vary according to the structure under which the charity is constituted.

The main responsibilities for those responsible for the governance of charities are:

- As **charity trustees**: they have the responsibility under charity law as trustees for the funds they are responsible for to see that they are properly applied, and to see that all the requirements of charities law are met.

- As **management committee members**: they plan, implement and oversee the charity's work programme, and have legal responsibilities under a wide variety of legislation – including employment law, health and safety at work law, etc.

- As **company directors**: for those charities constituted as companies under the Companies Acts or where they are directors of an associated trading company, to comply with the Companies Acts and other legislation affecting companies.

Whoever they are, they must also at all times:

- Operate within the constitution of the organisation,, which defines its purposes, their powers, and the procedures for running the organisation.

- Operate within the law.

The titles of those responsible for the affairs of the charity are not always used consistently. Thus the Directors of a charitable company may be referred to as Charity Trustees (which they are under the Charities Act), but the Chief Executive may be referred to as The Director.

For the purposes of this book, we have tried to be consistent, and use the terms as follows:

- **Charity Trustee** or **The Trustees**: This refers to those people who have the overall responsibility for running the charity. This includes the trustees of a charity constituted as a trust, the directors of a charity constituted as a company or an industrial and provident society, and the management committee of a charity constituted as an unincorporated association or society. They have both trustee responsibilities and management responsibilities. We use these terms when discussing matters that refer to all charities.

- **Directors**: This refers to the directors of a charitable company or any person occupying the position of director by whatever name called. Directors of companies have additional responsibilities under company legislation. We use this term for those situations which are relevant to those charities constituted as companies and for situations where the legislation also covers unincorporated associations. The Directors will normally also be the trustees of the charity.

- **Shadow Directors**: This refers to those people in accordance with whose directions or instructions the Directors are accustomed to act. They are not directors as such, but they have some of the responsibilities of directors, in that they may be held liable for wrongful trading.

- **Members**: This refers to the members of a charitable company who have each provided a guarantee (usually nominal) to the company in the event that the resources of the company are not sufficient to meet its obligations. Under insolvency law, the members of a company have certain rights (see Chapter 2). The term 'member' should not be confused with the membership of an organisation through some form of subscription scheme. Such 'members' are supporters or friends of the organisation. They may also be, but are not necessarily members of the company.

- **Insolvency Practitioner**: This refers to an individual having the necessary licence under the legislation to carry out liquidations and most other insolvency procedures.

Because charities are differently constituted, and because the registration, the accountability requirements, the insolvency procedures and the personal liabilities of those at the helm all vary according to how the organisation is constituted, we have tried throughout the book to show the particular situation as it will affect your organisation, but first you will need to know how your organisation is constituted.

INTRODUCTION

Solvency and insolvency

Insolvency is what happens when it goes wrong. At that stage, things move out of your control. **Solvency** is preventing your organisation ever getting near the insolvency zone. And **robustness** is the financial muscle and strength to ensure that the organisation is able to come through periods of financial difficulty.

Whether you are near to insolvency, or whether you think you might at some stage be so, or whether you are simply concerned to build a robust organisation that will never get near to being insolvent, the issue of insolvency is an important one. It is also important if you advise or fund charities or other voluntary organisations, for here you have the opportunity not just to give advice or support to keep them going in the short term, but to help give them the structures and the strategies to keep strong and healthy into the future.

Why insolvency is a problem

Insolvency (and the issue of solvency) is more than just a problem of the early 1990s recession – although the recession has created its own catalogue of insolvencies as much in the voluntary sector as in the business sector. Some charities have gone into liquidation or receivership; some have simply terminated when their grant has been cut. But there are other reasons why the issue of insolvency is important:

- The new **SORP 2 accounting requirements** impose greater reporting obligations on charities. This means that the state of the organisation's financial health will become that much more apparent to those reading the accounts. If you are unable to disguise a financial problem, you will find it that much harder to raise the money you need, thereby compounding the problem.

- The **1993 Charities Act** focuses on the responsibilities of charity trustees. Trustees faced with dwindling assets and growing liabilities will be concerned to do something about it. If the charity is an unincorporated body, then any encounter with insolvency will impose personal liabilities on the trustees to make good any deficit. If the charity is incorporated, under the Companies Act, the directors may lay themselves open to personal liability if they continue to operate whilst knowingly insolvent. Mere expectation that things will come right eventually may not be sufficient.

- The **changing funding patterns** of many charities create additional risks. For many, and this applies most of all to local service-providing voluntary organisations once funded wholly or very substantially from one large local authority grant, there is now a diversity of funding sources, growing competition for the readily available sources of funds, and more emphasis on earning money by sales of services. There is not only more risk, and therefore more need to have reserves to act as a buffer; but there may be a need to invest in development or invest in marketing, spending money now to generate income in the future.

- In the event of an **insolvency**, any actions will be judged with the benefit of hindsight and on the assumption that proper financial systems were in place (in the context of legal requirements and the special nature of the organisation).

The problems of insolvency

Not only is insolvency a problem, but it creates problems for the organisation. There are three zones of insolvency, each with its own consequences:

The organisation is technically no longer solvent or has been deemed to be insolvent. At this stage, events take over and those responsible for the organisation lose control. *Chapter 1* gives a legal perspective on insolvency. *Chapter 2* describes what happens when the organisation actually is insolvent. The main lesson is to do everything you can to avoid becoming insolvent in the first place.

The organisation is a going concern for at least the next year ahead and hopefully for the longer term. Here the concern shifts to developing and implementing management and financial strategies for the organisation which will ensure its continuing robustness and sustainability. *Chapters 7-9* discuss many of the steps which can be taken to achieve this.

The organisation is in the 'grey zone' somewhere between solvency and insolvency. Here it may be technically solvent, but it may also be financially weak or have poor prospects for the medium term. The danger of insolvency is a consideration that must be taken into account. *Chapters 3-6* look at the financial position from a number of different perspectives.

- The perspective of the **accountant** *(Chapter 3)* who is responsible for auditing the charity's accounts, for providing an **audit statement** which could qualify the accounts but more usually gives them a 'clean bill of health' and for providing management advice on the financial procedure and accounting processes. The auditor has an external role to examine the accounts, ensure compliance with accounting standards, report whether they give a true and fair picture of the financial position, and confirm the going concern status of the organisation.

- The perspective of the **financial administrator** *(Chapter 4)*, the employee or volunteer responsible for supervising or doing the bookkeeping and the charity's accounts and responsible for overseeing the financial position of the organisation and notifying the chief executive (or senior staff member) and the trustees (or management committee) if there are problems ahead.

- The perspective of the **trustees** (or members of the management committee, if the organisation is not a charity) *(Chapter 5)*. All trustees are responsible, but two are more responsible than the others – the treasurer who assumes a specific role for overseeing the charity's finances on behalf of the other trustees, and the chair who has the leadership role for the organisation. The trustees have two different perspectives. Their prime role is to act on behalf of the beneficiaries and to protect the charity's assets and resources for the purposes of the charity. As such they must take into account future needs and future beneficiaries. But they also have their own interests to protect – either because they are trustees of an unincorporated body and personally responsible for any liabilities it runs up, or because as directors of an incorporated body they must ensure that if they continue to trade they have the financial viability to do so.

- The perspective of the **Charity Commission** *(Chapter 6)*. The Commission is responsible for supervising charities in England and Wales, for seeing that the interests of beneficiaries are kept to the fore, for ensuring that the role of trustee does not create such burdens and liabilities that people no longer put themselves forward to serve as trustees, and for maintaining the reputation of the charity sector as a whole.

Chapter 7 discusses what to do if something needs to be done in a hurry. For organisations in the grey zone, the trustees and senior staff have a critical role to play. If they act swiftly and decisively they have a chance to turn the organisation around. If they fail to act, insolvency may loom.

Actual insolvency leads to winding up and failure. Potential insolvency also creates problems which will have an adverse effect on the ability of the organisation to function:

- If shortfalls in current income are met from accumulated reserves or capital, and the shortfalls continue, then not only will there be a continuing drain on resources, but investment income derived from reserves and unspent cash balances will reduce year by year, compounding the financial difficulties.

- If so much effort is being placed on getting the organisation through the period of difficulty and so much fundraising effort in scraping together the resources to survive in the short term, then the strategic development of the organisation and the development of its funding base for the longer term will be given a lesser priority.

- Any qualification of the 'going concern status' in the accounts will put the organisation's fundraising at risk. Some donors may not want to give to an organisation whose medium term viability appears in doubt, however good the services it is providing.

- Staff morale may decline if it appears that their jobs are at risk. They may want to spend time trying to protect their own future, rather than the organisation's.

- The personal liability of trustees in the event of failure may prompt some to resign or deter others from being drafted in to help.

When to be concerned

There are a number of different problems which can constitute insolvency. Each is different, and each will require different solutions:

- A **cash flow hole**. Expenditure is consistently exceeding income, and as resources get eaten up, the situation can only get worse.

- A **major grant failure**. Perhaps now or looming there is the prospect that a major part of the organisation's funding will be withdrawn. This can come about either as a result of an actual cut, or because a grants programme terminates or its grants criteria change so radically that it is no longer possible to apply (this happened for example with the demise of the Community Programme).

- The organisation has **negative net worth** – that is its assets do not cover its liabilities – and there is no prospect of the necessary funding appearing to cover the shortfall.

- The organisation does not have sufficient **liquid resources** available to cover its obligations. It may be asset rich, but if it cannot raise or borrow the cash needed to pay the bills, this can lead to action being taken by creditors.

- The organisation has **contingent liabilities** not backed by assets. For example, repairing obligations under a lease, or the obligations to employees consequent on their employment create contingent liabilities which must be accounted for and should be provided for.

- Wasting assets and equipment that there are not the **resources to replace**. If the organisation depends on these assets to continue providing a service, and if the assets are not being kept in a fit state, and if there are not the funds to replace the equipment at the end of its useful life, and if fundraising prospects are poor, then there will come a time when the organisation can no longer function effectively.

Organisations can become insolvent in any of these situations. If any are relevant to you now, or seen to be just around the corner, then you need to do something... now. You will usually have two jobs to do:

1. To address the **immediate problem** which may be to cut expenditure, to restructure the work, to bring in volunteers, to fundraise, to find additional users or customers, and

2. To develop a sound **long-term strategy** for operating the organisation successfully and for creating a sustainable stream of income to fund it.

PART 1

INSOLVENCY AND LIQUIDATION
SOLVENCY AND GOING CONCERN STATUS

The legal, accounting and financial considerations

CHAPTER 1
WHAT IS INSOLVENCY: A LEGAL PERSPECTIVE

BY STEPHEN LLOYD

What is insolvency?

Charities operate under a number of varying constitutional forms; **companies limited by guarantee or by shares**, societies **incorporated by Royal Charter**, **industrial and provident societies**, unincorporated **associations** or **trusts**. The law relating to insolvency has a different impact depending on how a charity is constituted. Where the charity is incorporated, the Insolvency Act 1986 will apply. This Act also applies to industrial and provident societies. However, only some 20,000 of the 170,000 or so registered charities are set up as limited companies. The vast bulk are unincorporated, whether they are constituted as trusts or unincorporated associations. Where unincorporated charities become insolvent, the liabilities pass to the trustees, and the bankruptcy laws (which apply to individuals) will apply where the trustees are unable to meet the liabilities of the charity.

The impact of insolvency varies depending on whether or not a charity is a limited liability company or an industrial and provident society or an unincorporated association or trust. Although, for example, the tests for insolvency refer to the Insolvency Act 1986 and its impact upon limited liability companies, the same principles apply, obviously, to unincorporated associations or trusts. Insolvency has different effects upon organisations depending upon how they are constituted, whether as companies or as unincorporated organisations. This differing impact is dealt with in various sections in this chapter.

In company law, which applies to all companies whether limited by guarantee or shares, 'insolvency' and 'insolvent' have no uniform or comprehensive meaning. Broadly speaking there are two separate tests to determine if a company is insolvent. These two tests are also used in relation to individual insolvency.

Tests of insolvency

There are a number of different tests which can be used to determine whether an organisation is insolvent.

The going concern test: the basis of this test is whether the company can pay its debts as they fall due. This is also known as the **cash flow test**. This test is applied in various cases:

(a) for the purposes of a declaration of insolvency (a prerequisite for the solvent winding up of a company) the directors have to state whether the company will be able to pay its debts in full plus interest over a twelve month period.

(b) Section 122(1)(f) of the Insolvency Act 1986 provides that a company may be wound up by order of the Court as insolvent if it is unable to pay its debts as they fall due.

Obviously this test may be used by the directors of a company who are concerned about its solvency to check on its financial health.

The balance sheet test: under this test, insolvency denotes the actual or anticipated deficiency of assets to meet the company's liabilities. This is reflected in Section 122(1)(f) Insolvency Act 1986 which provides a second ground for winding up a company as unable to pay its debts if the value of its assets is less than the amount of its liabilities, taking into account its contingent and prospective liabilities. Again, the directors may use this test to check on the company's financial health.

The major problem with the balance sheet test and its requirement that full account be taken of contingent and prospective liabilities is the inter-relationship with the 'going concern' test of calculating liabilities. Under the going concern test, it is assumed that a company will continue to trade, and therefore that liabilities which would crystallise should the company have ceased trading are not taken into account in assessing the company's actual or contingent liabilities. The going concern test is rather like a bicycle. So long as the cyclist maintains forward momentum, all is well. But if the rider loses impetus, the bicycle wobbles and falls over. Crash. So too with a company.

If a calculation of its assets and liabilities is made on the basis of the company ceasing to trade (the so called 'break up' basis) as compared with the going concern test, the effect on the company's balance sheet may well be enormous. Firstly, the value of the assets may be written down greatly – secondhand goods will almost certainly command a much lower price on the open market than their book value as stated in the company's accounts. Secondly, stopping trading will cause a number of major liabilities to appear and thus inflate the company's indebtedness.

Thirdly, bank borrowings which were used to fund the ongoing operation will have to be repaid.

For example:

• staff will be made redundant, thus triggering compensation payments for notice periods and redundancy;

• leasing companies who have hired out photocopiers, computers, cars or other equipment will terminate the contracts and demand all the future instalments due under the terms of the lease less a small discount to reflect early repayment;

- the landlord of leasehold premises will demand any undue rent and may slap in a claim for damages for breach of a covenant in the lease (e.g. to repair);
- claims may arise for breach of contract to deliver services.

If the balance sheet test is not calculated on a going concern method but on a break up basis, the results will almost inevitably be much worse, and the prospects of insolvency much greater. It is thus very important for directors to know whether a valuation is to be done on the going concern or the break up basis as the results will be very different. Directors may have a valuation prepared on the going concern basis provided that they reasonably consider that the company will be able to continue to trade. If on the other hand if they conclude that it is not reasonable to assume that the company will be able to continue to trade, they must have the valuation prepared on a break up basis.

The cash flow and balance sheet tests cannot be seen as a strict either/ or. The two may well impact on each other. Hence a deficiency of assets may eventually result in a cash flow crisis. Equally an adverse cash flow may force a company to sell off assets cheaply thereby causing the company to fail the balance sheet test.

The insolvency of unincorporated organisations: trusts

The debts of a limited company are its and its alone. If a company is insolvent, the limited company may be forced into insolvent liquidation. The directors of that company will not incur any personal liability for the debts of the company, except in limited circumstances *(see below)*.

The position is very different for an unincorporated association or a trust. In either case there is no separate entity with limited liability because a trust or an unincorporated association has no legal personality of its own. The debts of an unincorporated organisation are ultimately the responsibility of the charity trustees.

If a trust is sued for a debt, then it is the charity trustees' names which will appear on the writ. If a trust incurs an obligation, for example enters into a lease, it is the charity trustees' names which appear on the lease. Sections 50 to 62 of the Charities Act 1993 do allow charity trustees to incorporate the trustee body. But such incorporation does not affect the charity trustees' personal liabilities, as the charity itself remains unincorporated.

Many trust deeds contain an indemnity from the trust to the charity trustees for any liability properly incurred by them in the course of fulfilling their duties as trustee, such that the charity's funds can be used to pay these liabilities. But this indemnity is useless if the trust lacks the financial resources to honour it.

> ## Example:
>
> A school run by a trust closed down. The trust had insufficient reserves to meet its redundancy liabilities to the staff. The charity trustees were sued personally by the staff and each trustee had to pay £5,000 to meet the redundancy costs. The indemnity in the trust deed was useless.

If the trustees are held personally liable, the liability of the trustees is 'joint and several'. This means that all the trustees could be held equally liable or that the whole or a large part of the claim could be pursued against any one of the trustees. If the liabilities of the trust exceed the trustees' personal wealth the charity trustees could themselves be forced into personal bankruptcy.

A creditor may petition for the bankruptcy of an individual if the debtor owes a debt above a minimum of £750 and the debtor appears to be unable to pay that debt or appears to have no reasonable prospect of being able to pay that debt. A debtor appears to be unable to pay a debt if he or she has been served with a statutory demand, and more than three weeks have elapsed since the demand was served, and he or she has neither complied with the demand nor applied to have it set aside. A creditor can decide to sue only one of the body of trustees, 'picking off' the person deemed most likely to pay. The charity trustee who is forced to pay up has a right to petition the Court for a contribution from each of the other trustees for a proportionate part of the debt due. Under the Civil Liability (Contribution) Act 1978, the Court has the power to award in favour of one trustee against another a contribution of such amount as the Court considers to be just and equitable, having regard to the extent of the responsibility of that other trustee for loss. The Court may exempt any person from liability to make a contribution.

> ## Example:
>
> Trustee A is sued and pays £10,000 damages. The plaintiff does not sue the other trustees.
>
> There are four other trustees. A may seek an order from the Court to force the other trustees to contribute to A.
>
> If one of the trustees is unable to meet any contributions ordered by the Court (e.g. because he is insolvent) the other trustees will have to meet the liability of the bankrupt trustee equally amongst themselves.

The insolvency of unincorporated organisations: unincorporated associations

The members of the management committee of an unincorporated association are in the same position as the trustees of a charitable trust – they too are charity trustees – except for one difference. Under the rules of an unincorporated association, the members of the association, who elect the management committee may agree to indemnify the management committee members for liabilities properly incurred by them in serving on the management committee. It must be emphasised that the committee can only make the general members of the association personally liable if the constitution clearly gives them that power or if the members sanction the liability within the constitution.

In such circumstances if an unincorporated association is unable to pay its debts as they fall due or if its liabilities exceed its assets, ultimately the members of the association may be liable equally for the association's debts. However, a creditor will be entitled to sue the members of the management committee, who will be deemed to have been responsible for the running of the association. The members of the management committee will then have to seek indemnity from the members if this is appropriate.

Accounting requirements

By Section 41(2)(b) of the Charities Act 1993 the accounting records of a registered charity must contain 'a record of the assets and liabilities of the charity'.

This does not apply to companies which are charities. They are excluded by Section 41(5), but they must maintain identical accounting records by virtue of Section 221 Companies Act 1985 the wording of which is mirrored in Section 41. Nor does Section 41 apply to exempt charities (those charities that are exempt from having to register). They are excluded by Section 46(1) which makes it clear that they must continue to comply with the general obligation to keep accounts laid down by Section 36 of the 1993 Act.

The liabilities which a company must record are stated at paragraph 89 schedule 4 Companies Act 1985 'any liability or loss which is either likely to be incurred or certain to be incurred but uncertain as to amount or as to the date on which it will arise'. It seems likely that a similar test will apply for unincorporated charities under Section 41.

What happens when an organisation becomes insolvent?

The consequences of insolvency will depend on the form of the organisation. Different rules apply to limited companies and industrial and providential societies. For trusts, the claims will be pursued against the trustees and for associations against the management committee and possibly also the membership (as has already been described).

Liquidation of limited companies

If a company is insolvent, it will usually be forced into insolvent liquidation by a dissatisfied creditor who will petition the Court to have the company wound up on the grounds that it cannot pay its debts. This is established if the creditor has served a statutory demand for a minimum sum of £750, and the company has neglected to pay the sum or to secure it to the reasonable satisfaction of the creditor within three weeks. Equally a company is deemed to be unable to pay its debts if a company fails the balance sheet test (i.e. its liabilities outstrip its assets).

Alternatively to pre-empt the creditors the members can pass a special resolution (i.e. one passed by 75% of the members present and voting at a duly convened meeting on 21 days notice) to put the company into voluntary liquidation.

Whichever path is chosen a petition is presented to either the High Court in London or the appropriate County Court for the company to be wound up. The Court will, if it things fit, appoint a liquidator. This will either be the Official Receiver – who is a civil servant – or if there is a prospect of the liquidation being able to sustain the payment of professional fees – a private insolvency practitioner.

The liquidator's task is to gather in the assets of the insolvent company for the benefit of the creditors and pay them off in order of priority as follows. If there are insufficient assets to pay off for example the unsecured creditors in full, they are each paid a 'dividend' (a rather confusing word in the context) of say 10p for each £1 owed to them. The same would apply to the preferential creditors, if there are insufficient funds to pay them in full.

The creditors are not equal. There are four types of creditor who rank in order of payment as follows:

1. **Secured**: for example, a bank with a mortgage ('security') over an asset of the company;

2. **Pre-preferential**: the Liquidator's fees;

3. **Preferential**: these consist of PAYE, VAT, social security contributions, occupational pension scheme contributions and amounts due to employees for wages for the four months prior to the making of the winding up order or resolution to wind up (not exceeding £800 per employee), together with all arrears of holiday pay;

4. **Unsecured**: these are the ordinary debts which are not secured or preferential.

The liquidation process and the liquidator's role are described in much more detail in *Chapter 2*.

What are the assets of an insolvent charity?

Company law recognises that certain types of property held by an insolvent company will not be part of the assets of the company available for distribution among the creditors. This applies in particular to property held for third parties or in trust. It applies equally to property which has been charged, usually to secure borrowings made by a lender. This is of special relevance to charitable companies. The same points apply equally to in unincorporated organisation – assets held by it in trust for a third party may not be used to pay off the organisation's own debts.

Trust property can include items held in specific trust for another person.

Example 1:

Charity A (a limited company) and charity B have run a joint fundraising campaign. Charity A receives all the moneys but agrees to hold Charity B's share on trust for Charity B.

Charity A holds £20,000 of the proceeds which it is due to pay to Charity B.

Charity A goes into insolvent liquidation. The liquidator of Charity A could not use the moneys due to Charity B as they are held in trust for Charity B.

The position may well be different if the agreement between Charity A and Charity B is silent on the status of the moneys held by Charity A (where it does not stipulate that they are held in trust). In this case, Charity B would have to convince the liquidator that Charity A was a constructive trustee of the moneys – which may be difficult to prove.

Example 2:

Charity C, a grant making trust, has advanced £50,000 to Charity A in return for Charity A carrying out a specific piece of research.

Charity A (a limited company) goes into insolvent liquidation when £20,000 of the grant remains unspent.

Charity C can demand repayment of the moneys from the liquidator of Charity A on the basis of a constructive trust.

The position of Charity C will be much stronger and the constructive trust easier to establish if the grant moneys were kept in a separate bank account marked 'Charity C Grant Moneys Trust Account'.

Alternatively an account may be made in the charity's books entitled 'Grant Moneys Trust Account'. This is a less effective method of protecting Charity C's interest as although the accounts refer to the trust the cash will be in the general bank account of Charity A and may all have been spent. Hence Charity C will then have to hope that there are sufficient assets of Charity A available to repay the £20,000.

Permanent endowment

Section 96(3) of the Charities Act 1993 states that 'a charity shall be deemed to have a permanent endowment unless all property held for the purposes of the charity may be expended for those purposes without distinction between capital and income'.

Does property which is subject to permanent endowment cause any problem in the case of a charity becoming insolvent? The charity holds the permanent endowment on trust and applies any income deriving from it for the purposes of the charity. If the charity (being a company) goes into liquidation or (being unincorporated) faces insolvency, any assets which are permanent endowment will be held to form part of the general assets of the charity available for distribution among the creditors or to meet the charity's debts. Those assets will have to be realised in the normal way for the benefit of the creditors.

Administration of limited companies

British company law has long been criticised for being too simplistic in its treatment of insolvent companies. For many years it offered no means of nursing an insolvent company back to financial health, unlike in the United States where Chapter 11 of the Bankruptcy Code enables a company which is facing financial difficulties, to obtain the protection of the Court from its creditors.

To remedy this deficiency and building on the US experience, the Insolvency Act 1986 introduced the Administration Order. An Administration Order can be made:

- to ensure the survival of the company in whole or in part as a going concern; or
- to ensure a more advantageous realisation of the company's assets than would be the case in a winding up.

How to obtain an administration order

An Administration Order is made on a petition to either the relevant County Court or the High Court, backed up (usually) by the proposed administrator's report. If the Court makes an Administration order no steps can be taken against the company or its property (e.g. suing for a debt) except with the leave of the Court. No security (e.g. a mortgage) can be enforced against the company. In other words the company is in a court protected safe haven, immune from its creditors whilst it is nursed back to health by the administrator who has similar powers to a receiver (i.e. to buy and sell property and to manage the company's affairs) so long as the creditors agree to the administration. The powers of the directors are effectively suspended for the duration of the administration.

Bankruptcy of unincorporated associations and trusts

Although an unincorporated organisation can become insolvent, the consequences are very different from the insolvency of a limited company. There is no legal mechanism for the organisation itself to be put into liquidation or administration. If the unincorporated organisation lacks the resources to meet its liabilities, the burden will fall onto the trustees or members of the management committee personally. If they fail to meet those obligations, the creditor can sue them (or any of them) and petition to have them made bankrupt. If the petition is successful, the trustee's assets become vested in an individual appointed by the Court with the somewhat confusing title of 'Trustee in Bankruptcy'. The Trustee in Bankruptcy can be either a government official (the Official Receiver) or a private insolvency practitioner.

The Trustee in Bankruptcy, just like the liquidator of a limited company, is responsible for gathering in the bankrupt's assets and paying off the creditors. The order of priority for paying off the debts of a limited company applies equally to an individual. There is no legal provision for Administration in the case of an individual so he or she cannot trade his or her way back to solvency with the aid of the Court.

If individuals are made bankrupt, they lose all their assets; they cannot obtain credit or serve as a director of a company. If they are professionals (e.g. a solicitor or a Member of Parliament), they will lose that status. They are automatically discharged from the bankruptcy after three years, in normal circumstances.

On the other hand so as to avoid bankruptcy an individual debtor can try to strike a voluntary arrangement with his or her creditors. This can be achieved by getting 75% of the creditors (calculated by value) to vote to accept a compromise plan whereby the debtor agrees to pay a limited amount (e.g. 50p in the £) to each creditor over an agreed period in return for the creditors not making him or her bankrupt. This compromise binds all creditors (even if they voted against the plan) so that they cannot seek to bankrupt the debtor in respect of the debts which are subject to the voluntary arrangement.

The consequences of ignoring potential insolvency

The consequences of a charity becoming insolvent depend on its constitutional structure. If the charity is unincorporated, the liabilities of the charity will be borne by the charity trustees (which could ultimately result in personal bankruptcy). If the charity is a limited company or an industrial and provident society, its debts are the debts of the organisation and not of the directors or the members personally. In the case of a company limited by guarantee, the members will be liable to pay the guarantee they have given as members. The level of guarantee is stated in the charity's Memorandum and Articles of Association – this is usually only £1 but it may be more. This guarantee is only given by the members. It is not given by the directors (unless they are also members).

However, the protections of limited liability are not absolute. The directors of a limited company may lose the protections of limited liability and be made to contribute from their own personal assets towards the debts of an insolvent company in certain circumstances. It appears tat the members of the management committee of an industrial and provident society cannot be held personally liable under the doctrine of wrongful trading (see below) in Great Britain. The position is different in Northern Ireland. Wrongful trading does apply to industrial and provident societies in Northern Ireland.

Fraudulent trading

By Section 213 Insolvency Act 1985 on the application of the liquidator of a company the Court may order that any persons who were knowingly party to carrying on the business of the company with intent to defraud creditors must make a contribution to the company's assets.

Intent to defraud creditors must be proved and the onus of proof is on the liquidator. There must be evidence of actual dishonesty.

Example:

R v. Grantham (1984): It was held that an intent to defraud might be inferred if the person concerned obtained credit when he knew there was no good reason for thinking that funds would be available to pay the debt when it became due or shortly afterwards.

AND

Re a Company (No. 001418 of 1988): A company went into insolvent liquidation owing £212,681. The Court held on the facts that there had been fraudulent trading. It ruled that a person was knowingly party to the business of the company having been carried on with intent to defraud creditors if:

(a) at the time when debts were incurred by the company, he had no good reason for thinking that funds would be available to pay those debts when they became due or shortly afterwards; and

(b) there was dishonesty involving real moral blame according to current notions of fair trading.

The Chairman, managing director and major shareholders had to pay £156,000 to the creditors.

It should be noted that it is not only the directors who can be made liable for fraudulent trading. For an insolvent charitable company, in addition to the charity trustees, the employees could be made liable for fraudulent trading (if proven).

Wrongful trading

This is a new form of civil liability, introduced by the Insolvency Act 1986 to counter criticisms that fraudulent trading was too difficult to prove and creditors were suffering due to the negligence of directors. Its object is to cover cases where the persons concerned have failed to exercise sufficient diligence in monitoring the company's affairs and in taking corrective action when insolvency loomed but have not acted in bad faith or fraudulently.

Wrongful trading applies to directors and to shadow directors. For the purposes of the Companies Acts a director is anyone who occupies the position of a director, by whatever name called. It is not necessary in order to be treated as a director, for the director to have been registered as such at Companies

House. Hence this could include say a Chief Executive who was accustomed to running the organisation. A 'shadow director' is a person in accordance with whose directors or instructions the directors of the company have been accustomed to act. This does not apply where the directors act on advice given to them by that person in a professional capacity. In the case of a charitable company it is possible that a charismatic and powerful chief executive (who almost invariably will not be a trustee) could be treated as a shadow director.

Wrongful trading is established if the Court concludes that at some time before the company went into insolvent liquidation the director(s) or shadow director(s) *knew* or *ought to have concluded* that there was no reasonable prospect that the company would avoid going into insolvent liquidation, unless the Court is satisfied that the director took every step with a view to minimising the potential loss to the company's creditors as he or she ought to have taken.

The test is an objective one. The director must act as a reasonably diligent person having both the director's own knowledge, skills and experience and the general knowledge, skill and experience that may *reasonably* be expected of a person carrying out the same functions as the director. The standard expected will vary from one case to another. In *Re Produce Marketing Consortium Limited (1989)*, the Judge held that the expertise expected of a director is much less extensive in a small company in a modest way of business with simple accounting procedures and equipment than in a large company with sophisticated procedures.

This is of particular relevance to charity trustees. The trustees of charitable companies are almost invariably non-executive directors. They may meet rarely (say 4 times a year) and may be very dependent on the professional full-time staff. They must trust their staff. This is entirely fair and a recent case has shown that a director is entitled to trust persons in a position of responsibility until there is reason to distrust them *(Norman v. Theodore Goddard 1991)*. What standard of duty will the Court expect of charity trustees in a wrongful trading case? Will it be a lower standard than that of a full-time employee who is also a director (which is almost invariably the case in the private sector)? So far (to the writer's knowledge) no case of wrongful trading has been brought against directors of a charitable company but it would be reasonable to argue for a lower standard than for a full-time employee director. It should be emphasised that a person with financial or legal skills or a financial function (for example, the treasurer) would be judged on this basis and thus will be at greater risk.

It should also be noted that Section 727 Companies Act 1985 provides that in any proceedings for 'negligence, default, breach of duty or breach of trust' against any officer of a company the Court may wholly or partly relieve that person of responsibility as it thinks fit if the director has acted honestly and reasonably and if having regard to all the circumstances he or she ought fairly to be excused of responsibility. It has been held that

Section 727 does not apply to wrongful trading. In other words if a director is found to be guilty of wrongful trading he or she cannot look to Section 727 to be exonerated from liability.

There is a similar provision in relation to unincorporated organisations in Section 61 of the Trustees Act 1925. This gives the Court the power to relieve a trustee wholly or partly from personal liability if it appears that the trustee has acted honestly and reasonably and ought fairly to be excused for a breach of trust. This provision does to excuse a trustee of an unincorporated charity from liability to creditors of that charity. Section 61 only applies to a breach of trust. The personal liability of a charity trustee for the debts of the charity does not arise from any breach of trust by the trustee.

Looming insolvency – the practical implications

If insolvency looms for a charity the best course of action for the charity trustees will vary according to the organisation's constitutional structure.

The implications for unincorporated organisations

As the debts and obligations of an unincorporated organisation are the personal liability and responsibility of the charity trustees (if the charity has insufficient assets to meet the debts and obligations), the primary aim of the trustees will be to minimise the build-up of debts and liabilities and to increase the assets by raising cash. But if attempts to generate income or cash fail then, in view of their personal risk, charity trustees may be keen to run down the organisation so as to minimise the chance of their incurring personal debts or even bankruptcy or being accused of breach of trust. On the other hand, by closing down new liabilities will crystallise. Moreover, closing down is easier said than done. Many charities will have long-term liabilities (e.g. a lease of a building) which it may prove impossible to assign. Hence the trustees may find themselves obliged to continue to pay rent and service charge even after the charity has ceased to operate and if the charity lacks the means to pay these costs the trustees will have to meet them personally. The advice about monitoring the charity's financial position and meeting regularly given for companies (see below) applies equally to an unincorporated organisation.

The implication for companies

In the case of a limited company the charity trustees will be anxious to ensure that the protections of limited liability are not lost. That means avoiding any allegation that the charity trustees have been guilty of wrongful trading or breach of trust.

Charity trustees must be able to show that they took all reasonable steps to minimise the loss to the company's creditors. This means in terms of practicalities that if they knew or ought to know that there is no reasonable prospect of avoiding insolvent liquidation the charity trustees must:

1. Recognise that their primary duty is no longer to fulfil the objects of the charity but to act in the best interests of the creditors. Hence they should seek not to incur further liabilities or expend money on charitable purposes but rather should endeavour to pay off the creditors. It may seem inappropriate for a charity to refuse to pay, for example, a grant to a beneficiary and instead use the moneys thus saved to pay the leasing charges for a photocopier, but the charity trustees' duty when they are aware of potential insolvency of the charity is to act in the best interests of the creditors – even if it means failing to act in the interests of the beneficiaries.

    The dilemma which the charity trustees face in such circumstances is difficult. They must be neither cowardly nor rash. They must not rush into liquidation (which might damage the interests of the creditors) nor must they plough on in insouciant disregard of the potential damage to creditors. They must not be carried away by the idea that because the charity fulfils a noble cause that this allow them to ignore their legal obligations to creditors. Nor should trustees succumb to the inherent optimism of many that, in the words of Mr Micawber 'something will turn up'. To protect the charity trustees from a claim of wrongful trading their actions must have been reasonable as viewed from the standpoint of the reasonable director. Belief in a possibility or trusting in providence (cynical though this may sound) is not regarded by sceptical British judges as being reasonable.

2. Ensure that they have appropriate written legal and financial advice, so that they can show that they acted responsibly. Such advice should be given to all the trustees. It is not sufficient for it to be given to the chair or chief executive; trustees should ensure that advice is passed on to all trustees, so that together they can make an informed decision. Equally, the adviser should try to ensure that this is done.

3. Hold prompt and regular meetings to show that they took matters seriously and acted with the interests of the creditors in mind. This might mean – if time is short – that charity trustees have to meet on a weekend!

4. Ensure that proper and detailed minutes are kept of all their meetings so that there is an adequate 'paper trail' to show how decisions were reached. Provided decisions are made carefully and with the benefit of professional advice (assuming of course that the charity has the financial resources to pay for such advice!) a Court will be reluctant to substitute with the benefit of hindsight its own commercial

judgement for that of the charity trustees, unless it considers that no reasonable director could have concluded that the action taken was in the interest of the company.

The concerns of Charity Commission

If a charity becomes insolvent and creditors are unpaid there is a good chance of adverse press publicity or a complaint being made to a Member of Parliament or to the Charity Commission. In each case this could trigger an investigation by the Charity Commissioners into the conduct of the charity's affairs.

The Commissioners act here to protect the interests of the beneficiaries and potential beneficiaries of the charity. If the inquiry concludes that the charity trustees have been negligent in their conduct of the charity's affairs the Commissioners have the power to petition the Court for an order that the trustees make a contribution from their own assets to the charity to compensate it for loss suffered as a result of the breach of trust by the trustees. Negligence can constitute a breach of trust.

This can apply to any charity howsoever constituted, whether incorporated as a company or unincorporated. Limited liability gives the charity trustees no protection here.

Example:

A charity lends £250,000 to its trading company. The trading company becomes insolvent. The charity is forced to write off the loan. As a result it fails the balance sheet test and the loss of the cash means it also fails the cash flow test.

The charity ceases its activities as it is insolvent. The Charity Commission concludes that the investment by the charity in the company was negligent and seeks to recover the moneys lost from the charity trustees personally.

Although this train of events has never yet happened (to the writer's knowledge) such a scenario is perfectly possible.

This example illustrates again the need for the charity trustees to have proper minutes of all meetings and decisions so that, if investigated, they can show that their decisions were fair and reasonable.

The consequences of insolvency

The following illustrate some consequences of insolvency:

Uncompleted contracts

The other party to the contract will have a claim for breach of contract if a charity ceases to deliver its contractual obligations due to insolvency. In the case of a limited company this claim will be made against the liquidator. The claimant will be one of the unsecured creditors of the company. Hence the chance of the claimant recovering much by way of damages is remote. In the case of an unincorporated charity the position is different. If the contract did not contain a clause limiting the trustees' liability, the claimant will be able to sue any or all of the trustees personally.

Employment rights of employees

Certain sums due to employees (up to four months arrears of wages plus accrued holiday pay) are preferential so that if the charity (being a limited company) becomes insolvent the employees claim in the liquidation for these sums will rank in priority to the ordinary creditors. If the charity is unincorporated and action is brought against the trustees personally which forces any or all of them into personal bankruptcy, the same rules concerning preference apply. However, it should be noted that an employees' entitlement to a redundancy payment on the termination of his employment is not a preferential debt. Employees rank as normal, unsecured creditors insofar as their claims for redundancy payments are concerned.

The Department of Employment covers various liabilities of insolvent employers out of the National Insurance Fund. The fund will cover the following claims by employees:

- not more than eight weeks' arrears of pay;
- the net of tax salary for or in lieu of the minimum statutory notice period;
- holiday pay for periods not exceeding six weeks due during the twelve months preceding the insolvency;
- statutory redundancy payments.

All of these entitlements are restricted to a maximum weekly pay rate of £705 currently.

It is doubly hard for employees of charities (having already been made redundant) to receive a reduced or delayed redundancy payment or to have to go to the lengths of suing the trustees personally for their redundancy compensation. Some charities take out redundancy insurance to meet redundancy costs, so that the charity trustees and the staff can rest assured that if insolvency strikes the employees will receive their redundancy pay. The cost of insurance will vary according to the number of employees, the length of their service and the level of the anticipated redundancy payments.

Transfer of undertakings

If a charity (Charity A) seeks to transfer its assets to another charity (Charity B), by virtue of the Transfer of Undertakings (Protection of Employment) Regulations 1981, the staff employed by Charity A immediately before the transfer will transfer automatically to being employed by Charity B; with all their accrued employment rights which they can now enforce against Charity B. Their employment rights attach, like barnacles to a ship, to the assets transferred. These Regulations were introduced as a result of a European Community Directive and in Great Britain were initially limited to the transfer of a 'commercial venture'. Hence it could be argued that the Regulations did not apply to a transfer of assets between two charities as these are not 'commercial ventures'. However this argument was overruled by a decision of the European Court of Justice which makes it clear that a transfer of any undertaking (whether or to of a commercial venture) is within the scope of the original European Directive. This is now expressly stated by Section 33(2) Trade Reform and Employment Rights Act 1993.

A final word of advice

The insolvency of a charity can expose charity trustees to potential personal liabilities – even in the case of incorporated charities. Trustees should therefore continually monitor the financial health of their charity. If insolvency looms, they should not stick their heads, ostrich like, in the sand, hoping that the problems will go away or that someone else will sort things out. They should address the problems and take appropriate professional advice sooner rather than later. Drifting or doing nothing may only exacerbate the problems.

CHAPTER 2

WHAT HAPPENS WHEN AN ORGANISATION IS INSOLVENT

BY PETER GOTHAM

This section explains the likely course of events if an organisation becomes insolvent. We discuss in detail the steps through which an insolvent organisation will pass so that the reader can understand the process. Short case studies are used to illustrate specific points.

The term 'Director(s)' is used as in the Companies Act, the Insolvency Act, the Directors Disqualification Act, etc. to refer to directors of charitable companies and other incorporated voluntary organisations. The directors might be called 'trustees' or 'management committee members'. In an unincorporated voluntary organisation, the committee members or trustees have the same role. Other people in control of an organisation, such as employees with an important managerial or financial role, may also be considered legally to have the same responsibilities as directors, trustees or committee members.

Signs that all is not well

Insolvency does not arrive overnight. But the signs of an impending insolvent situation need to be recognised. Sometimes there is one major cause, such as the withdrawal of an important source of funding, but generally the signs are less clear. If cash flow problems are gradually increasing, you will find that:

- excuses have to be given more and more often for late payment of bills
- PAYE and VAT arrears creep up
- pay rises cannot be implemented
- posts go unfilled
- short-time working is adopted

and all the time tension rises. Often some committee members vote themselves off the management committee because they are unwilling to get involved, which causes problems in itself.

If steps are not taken to address the problems, then:

- writs will begin to arrive

This is followed perhaps by:

- judgement debts going unsatisfied
- statutory demands being received, or
- distraint being levied or 'walking possession' being taken of assets

It may even reach the stage of:

- petitions to have the organisation wound-up being issued
- physical threats to staff or management committee members by those seeking payment of their claims (who could be in an equally desperate condition). Any actual incidents should be reported immediately to the police, who will take action to prevent a recurrence.

The organisation is probably insolvent – what do you do?

If you believe that the organisation is probably insolvent, then the first decision is obviously to confirm that there is no practical way of working through the problems without adopting an insolvency procedure. The chapters in this book on the legal aspects of insolvency *(Chapter 1)* and on insolvency from different financial standpoints *(Chapters 3-6)* will be helpful in understanding this problem and deciding what to do about it.

Insolvency is the end of the line. It is likely that the organisation's accountant or solicitor will be involved at this stage; either is likely to be able to recommend an appropriate insolvency practitioner (IP). All insolvency practitioners are licensed by a professional body or by the Department of Trade and Industry (DTI). An IP can only accept appointment if he or she is independent of the insolvent organisation and of its directors or committee members.

Types of insolvency procedure

If the IP agrees that the organisation is insolvent and that some form of insolvency procedure is called for, the next question is 'what to do?' There are several options. The most common procedures are:

- **Creditors' Voluntary Liquidation**. This is the most used procedure and what we assume will happen for most of this chapter. In this procedure, the creditors have the power to overturn the directors' choice of liquidator and supervise the liquidation.
- **Compulsory Liquidation**. Here the organisation is forced into involuntary liquidation by a creditor. The courts supervise this procedure.
- **Informal (negotiated) Arrangement**. The situation still requires resolution, but creditors are open to negotiation to come to a solution which all parties agree as practicable and reasonable in the circumstances.

The creditors' voluntary liquidation route can be used by companies limited by guarantee, by companies limited by shares and by industrial and provident societies.

Practically any type of incorporated body can be forced into compulsory liquidation. An unincorporated association not formed with a view to profit would, however, have to be dealt with by a Court Appointed Receiver.

Unincorporated associations cannot go into creditors' voluntary liquidation – but can negotiate an informal arrangement. This avoids the costs of a formal liquidation, but is much more difficult to organise and can easily fall apart – probably leading to personal action against the members of the committee – perhaps through the appointment of a Court Appointed Receiver.

In certain circumstances, one of the following procedures may be applicable:

- **Receivership**, when a creditor who has registered a charge secured on part or all of the organisation's property appoints an insolvency practitioner to take control of the company.

- **Administration Order**, when an insolvent organisation is put under the protection of the court. This is done so that the problems can be resolved in an orderly fashion. The administration costs involved mean that it is only useful in the case of large organisations.

- **Company Voluntary Arrangement**, which is a formal procedure similar to the informal arrangement procedure. The costs involved mean that this too is generally only useful for larger companies.

- **Court Appointed Receivership**, which is a general sweeping-up procedure that can be applied in a wide range of circumstances against any legal body. The objects of the receivership and the powers of the receiver are laid down on a case by case basis by the court. As the court lays down the objects of the appointment of the receiver and that person's powers, the rules and procedures referred to in this chapter may not directly apply. The general law on offences, creditors' rights, employee rights and other areas of concern does, however, generally apply.

These procedures are not referred to in any detail in the rest of this chapter.

Creditors' Voluntary Liquidation

The sequence of events for a creditors' voluntary liquidation (for an incorporated organisation) is as follows:

- The directors decide to call meetings of members and creditors.

- The members' meeting resolves to place the company into liquidation and to nominate a liquidator (at which point the organisation is in liquidation). The creditors' meeting then hears a report of the background, the likely value of assets and the extent of the probable liabilities. The directors' conduct is open to question at the meeting.

- The creditors' meeting then decides who to appoint as liquidator.

Generally the prospective liquidator deals with the actual administration of convening meetings in liaison with directors and staff. This includes sending notices to members and creditors with proxy forms so as to give members and creditors the opportunity to vote, even if they are not attending the meeting, *and* (this is important) where voting on behalf of an organisation to ensure that the person authorised to vote on behalf of the organisation has authority to do so. Proxy forms have to be completed and returned to enable a person to vote at the meeting on behalf of their organisation. Individuals who personally are creditors can attend and vote without returning a proxy form. Creditors' meetings also have to be advertised in the *London Gazette* and two appropriate publications. The prospective liquidator will need considerable assistance from the directors and staff to prepare the information needed for the meetings.

Between convening and holding the meetings

It is particularly important at this stage that the directors act in the awareness that the assets, including bank balances, should now be used in the interests of the creditors only, and that no further credit should be taken and no assets should be sold. This is in complete contrast with a going concern charity, where the directors have to act wholly in the interests of the beneficiaries of the charity (as defined in the objects clause in the constitution). The directors should be aware of the risks of paying some creditors before the majority ('preference') and indeed of continuing to operate whilst insolvent ('wrongful trading').

It should be stressed that there is a risk of breach of the Insolvency Act if assets are used other than in the interests of the creditors *as a whole*. Payment of some creditors and not of others could constitute a 'preference' under the Act.

Chapter 1 deals with wrongful trading in some detail.

A practical view should be taken in order that the assets are protected and the meetings are convened in the most efficient fashion. The directors need to work closely with the nominated liquidator during this period, but the directors, in law, remain in post and in control. In many circumstances it may be appropriate that:

- Employees continue in post until the meetings.
- Premises are still occupied, with electricity, gas and telephone services remaining connected and in use.
- Consumable supplies are obtained for cash. If paid for by cheque or credit, these will create liabilities which can only be met alongside the other liabilities of the organisation, and could lay the Directors open to personal claims for fraudulent trading.
- Perishable goods be sold. Any trading can continue (if for a profit *and* without obtaining credit).

- Assets be sold to enable the meetings to be properly convened or to raise cash to protect the majority of the assets, for example in order to pay insurance premiums.

The meetings

For practical reasons the meetings of members and creditors are generally held on the same day unless either:

- The organisation needs to go into liquidation before the creditors' meeting can be convened so that a liquidator can be in post quickly. This is very rare and is unlikely to be possible in a membership organisation.

or:

- The members' meeting has to be called outside the times and days allowed for the creditors' meeting – for instance in the evening or at the weekend.

or:

- There is some doubt as to whether the members' meeting is likely to be quorate (have a sufficient attendance) or whether it will agree to placing the organisation in liquidation. In these cases it is sometimes appropriate to allow time for the convening of an adjourned members' meeting before the date of the creditors' meeting, or even to allow time to notify the creditors that the members have decided *not* to place the company into liquidation.

The members' meeting must be convened and run in accordance with the rules of the organisation.

The law prescribes detailed rules as to how the creditors' meeting should be conducted, and when and where it can be held – as set out in the Insolvency Act 1986 (IA) and Insolvency Rules 1986 (IR).

In broad outline, a director acts as formal chair of the meeting but, in practice, the nominated liquidator runs the meeting and ensures that the law is complied with.

A formal report is given of the statutory position, the financial history and the events leading to the meeting. An estimated **statement of affairs** is presented showing estimated realisable values for the assets and expected claims from creditors – including staff claims and claims in respect of termination of equipment and property leases. Other reports such as extracts from the accounts, an estimated deficiency account (calculating estimated losses since the last balance sheet was prepared) and summaries of movement on the bank accounts are also often presented. Finally a list of creditors with the expected value of their claims is given to the meeting.

Each liquidation is slightly different, but the creditors' meeting is often one of the most unpleasant occasions for the director(s) who attend(s) – only one director is *obliged* by law to do so. Quite understandably the creditors can get very upset and blame the director for the scale of their losses. The prospective liquidator often has the role of keeping the meeting to the point and bringing it to a constructive conclusion.

The election of the liquidator is by majority vote by value of creditors present in person or by proxy. The meeting will also decide on whether a 'liquidation committee' of three or five creditors should be elected to represent the creditors during the course of the liquidation.

The results of the meeting are circulated to all creditors, as well as being advertised in appropriate publications and in the *London Gazette*. Creditors are requested to make their claims to the elected liquidator, and formal notices of the situation are filed at Companies House. A sworn copy of the statement of affairs and list of creditors is also filed at Companies House.

The liquidator now takes control of the company and the directors cease to have any powers. They are, however, under a duty to co-operate with the liquidator.

After the meeting

After the creditors' meeting, the liquidator has certain tasks to carry out and can generally use what assets are available to carry these out. This can mean that very few funds are available to pay the 'unsecured creditors' any dividend on what is owing them.

The job of the liquidator is to:

- **Realise all available assets**.
- **Agree the claims of the creditors**, if there is likely to be money available to meet these. The payment to creditors is known as a dividend, expressed as so many pence in the pound. If there is unlikely to be a dividend, the claims are often just noted for future reference.
- **Investigate the affairs of the company** and report on the conduct of the directors to the Department of Trade and Industry (DTI). The DTI deals with matters relating to the possible disqualification of directors. The liquidator may also take legal action against some or all of the directors.

As part of the processes outlined above, there are very detailed rules about the administration of the case, the records to be kept, and the returns that need to be made to the Registrar of Companies.

As has been indicated, the administration of the case involves certain basic work. The extent of any further work, whether in pursuing claims to assets or investigating the past, can depend a great deal on what funds are available. This fact is often difficult for people who are new to the process to understand. They are surprised that the liquidator often has to restrict the work to only those activities where there are sufficient resources to pay for the work being done.

The actual liquidation will often take a year or two to complete. This process can seem to drag on, but it is one of those situations where everything is restricted to the speed of the slowest. This can be the result of delays in the Inland Revenue agreeing their claims, delays with a debtor agreeing to pay money owed to the organisation, or problems in investigating the records. Throughout the liquidation process, there are periodic reports to any liquidation committee formed and to annual meetings to which all creditors are invited.

While this is happening, the organisation will have closed, the work once carried on will stop, the assets will have been sold, and the team of staff and directors will have disbanded. Another community resource will have been lost. This can leave a gap in the provision of services that will not be filled. From the point of view of the directors, the creditors and the community, the prospect of liquidation is something to avoid.

Employees

The employees are often laid off before the creditors' meeting, although they may continue in post until this time. Obviously, however, they are aware of their impending dismissal, and this situation can create another area of difficulty for the directors.

The employees have often worked hard, maybe even without pay, to keep the organisation going. They have frequently borne the brunt of negotiations with creditors, including the Inland Revenue and possibly Customs and Excise (the VAT authority). The situation now has to be faced that the efforts put in by the staff (as well as by the volunteers and the committee) have not been sufficient to stave off liquidation, and the consequence of the liquidation is that their employment will be terminated.

Case study 1: Problems for directors

An old-established charity in the care field bought its property in the 1970s for use as a centre for service provision. In the 1980s this property was revalued at £1,000,000. On the basis of this valuation the organisation's bankers were happy to lend an amount that gradually crept up to £350,000 by 1991.

These funds were used to develop the service at the centre, and charging local authorities for the services so provided. The cash also covered mounting losses on the service.

By late 1992, the directors were sufficiently concerned about the accumulating losses to get a professional opinion on the value of the building. They were staggered to find that the fall in the property market, together with local planning changes, gave the centre an open-market value of only about £140,000.

Liquidation followed, and the directors became at risk of prosecution under the directors disqualification legislation, or even of being sued by the liquidator for wrongful trading. The argument was that the value of the property was so important to their financial strategy that they should have considered much earlier that it might not be sufficient to cover the loan and other liabilities.

Employee rights

Employee rights are partly based on their contracts – but payment of contractual obligations depends on the asset realisations and order of priority ('ranking') of claims (*see Creditors' entitlements below*). In addition, payment by the liquidator from the company's funds will generally take some time as it depends on realising the assets and on agreeing the claims.

Generally a more reliable source of funds for ex-employees is via the Employment Protection (Consolidation) Act. Here the employees' statutory entitlement in respect of arrears of pay, pay in lieu of notice, redundancy and holiday pay is met by the Department of Employment (DE). The DE is then entitled to claim on the assets realised by the liquidator to the extent to which it has paid the staff claims. The term used for this is that the DE 'stands in the shoes' of the employees to that extent.

What this means is that the DE takes over (some of) the employees' rights, but the rights of the DE to claim in the liquidation are only the same as the employees originally had.

Creditor entitlements

Claims will be ordered into several groups. The most important are:

- **Secured claims**: These are claims which are secured by a mortgage or charge document against specific assets owned by an incorporated organisation. To be effective these 'charges' have to be registered at Companies House for a limited company, or with the Registrar of Friendly Societies for an industrial and provident society. There is an important distinction between fixed charge assets where specific assets are covered by the charge, and floating charge assets, where there is a general charge over a class of assets. The whole area is quite complicated and does not follow apparently common sense rules.

- **Preferential claims**: These are laid down by statute to be:
  recent PAYE arrears
  recent VAT arrears
  certain staff claims including some arrears of pay and holiday pay.

- **Unsecured** or **general claims**: These will include staff claims not determined as preferential, including claims for redundancy entitlements. The majority of claims fall into this category.

- **Deferred claims**: These are generally only share capital liabilities which do not apply in the case of companies limited by guarantee or industrial and provident societies.

The order of priority in meeting claims is:

1. **Fixed charge creditors**, and the costs of realising fixed charge assets. This is restricted to the value of the fixed charge assets realised.

2. **Costs of administering** the liquidation.

3. **Preferential creditors** from any surplus on fixed charge claims and from any other assets.

4. **Floating charge creditors** from any unused 'floating charge' assets.

5. **Unsecured creditors** from any funds available after the fixed charge, preferential and floating charge claims have been dealt with.

6. **Deferred claims**.

Any particular payment will often be a dividend *pro rata*, expressed in terms of a certain number of pence in the pound.

Retention of title

Before an asset is available to be sold, ownership may have to be established. This is a complicated area. In some cases goods are supplied and sold, but the supplier retains ownership until they are paid for. This practice is known as 'Retention of Title' (RoT). This is often a matter of dispute in commercial cases, but is less likely to affect 'not for profit' companies.

Compulsory liquidations

A compulsory liquidation is a winding-up under the supervision of the court. The process generally starts when a creditor issues a formal legal notice called a **statutory demand**. If this is not properly dealt with, there are grounds to issue a **petition** to wind up the company. When the court has made a 'Winding-up Order' a civil service official called the **Official Receiver** generally steps in as liquidator. This official can be replaced by a private sector liquidator if one is willing to act. This normally happens if there are assets to pay the liquidator (or creditors willing to foot the bill), or if there is a great public interest in the case.

The procedure after the appointment of the liquidator is similar to that after a liquidator is appointed in a creditors voluntary liquidation. One difference is that the Official Receiver will deal with the investigation of the conduct of the directors or committee members, even when a private sector liquidator takes over the rest of the case.

It is generally considered that a compulsory liquidation is a less efficient process for the creditors, if only because of the obvious lack of continuity and delays caused as a result. It is also generally seen as being a greater humiliation and blot on the copybook of the directors or committee members involved.

Informal arrangements

An informal arrangement involves contacting all creditors and agreeing their share of the available assets. The agreement of *all* the creditors is needed for this procedure. A lot of hard work is necessary to achieve this while the creditors are left in a very exposed position.

Case study 2: Hidden problems

A small charity has been operating for some years. Gradually the situation has evolved so that the staff are effectively running the project. Originally established as an unincorporated association, the organisation changed its legal structure to a limited company just over three years before the major source of funding was withdrawn.

The staff looked into the situation and reported that the reserves were just enough to pay staff their contractual entitlements and to wind up tidily. On the basis of this information, the management committee decided, subject to taking professional advice, that the staff should be given their contractual notice and paid their entitlements and that the creditor liabilities which had been identified should be met.

It turned out that the lease to the premises had been taken on while the charity was unincorporated. This meant that the original trustees, who had long since moved on, could be held responsible for the cost of any dilapidations when the premises were given up.

This news, and a realisation that the termination clauses on the photocopier lease were onerous, caused the committee to reconsider its position. It transpired, however, that the co-ordinator had written cheques for the redundancy entitlement, and the treasurer had 'misunderstood' the committee's decision and had signed the cheques.

A breakdown in relations between staff and the committee followed. The staff became careless with security at the premises and vandals got in. It then turned out that the insurance had been allowed to lapse.

The final straw was the realisation that two committee members had personally guaranteed the photocopier lease.

This story illustrates the problems that can be caused by poor management control. It may seem an extreme case, but it is quite feasible. It serves to identify a number of possible hidden problems, for example:

- That there may be obligations in respect of leases that have been assigned;
- That reliance on verbal assurances from local authority officers that obligations would not be enforced may not be sufficient;
- That reliance on the value of a freehold to justify continued operation despite ongoing losses will only create a bigger problem later on.

The possible problems are endless.

Case Study 3: Compulsory liquidation

A community centre had been operating for some years using a local firm of accountants to prepare the accounts. The Inland Revenue carried out an inspection which threw up considerable problems.

It turned out that the bookkeeper had made some mistakes in his calculations three years earlier, which resulted in an understatement of the PAYE liabilities of some £10,000. As if this was not enough, it also was apparent that the cleaners had been paid on a casual basis, and PAYE and National Insurance had not been deducted and accounted for as required.

These problems warned the Inland Revenue to look into the records in more detail. They came across the payments to summer holiday playscheme workers and to casual staff who had occasionally been used for extended periods, when the full-staff were on holiday, or were off on maternity or long-term sick leave. As with the cleaners, PAYE had not been deducted on these payments. The total PAYE liability now amounted to £30,000.

The committee tried to negotiate the payment of the arrears over time but they did not take professional advice. They had heard quite wrongly that the Inland Revenue *had* to accept any reasonable offer to pay off PAYE arrears. They therefore paid over all their cash reserves amounting to £5,000 and offered to pay the balance at £200 per month. Not counting the interest constantly accruing on the outstanding balance, it would have taken more than 10 years to clear the liability.

The Collector of Taxes sent several letters explaining that this arrangement would not be satisfactory, which were not replied to. The Collector finally lost patience and issued a Statutory Demand which was not properly dealt with.

In the end, an organisation that might have been able to work something out with the Inland Review was wound up. It was then too late to retrieve the position, and the committee, the employed staff, and the local community all lost out.

The use of appropriate professional support early on would have prevented the PAYE problems getting so large, or later on might have helped retrieve the situation. The situation should have been picked up early on when the accounts were audited, and this underlines the importance of using an auditor who understands the voluntary sector, takes an interest in your organisation and can identify and help you deal with important issues such as non-payment of PAYE or VAT.

Case Study 4: An informal arrangement

A small community business had been trading for over 10 years, paying low wages and with a low asset base. In fact this unincorporated association had been insolvent for some years. It had been able to keep trading because nobody had wanted to put the organisation into compulsory liquidation, and because of the energy and commitment of the members.

The members ran out of energy and gradually moved on leaving one sole survivor – Sarah. Sarah wanted to sort things out, but as the business was not incorporated, she could not arrange for a creditors' voluntary liquidation. A compulsory liquidation was a possibility, but this could be cumbersome and an inefficient means of dealing with the realisation of the assets. In addition it would mean that the members' conduct would be reviewed by an unsympathetic system with the possibility of trouble for them because of the long period of their insolvent trading.

Sarah decided to try and sell the assets and to negotiate termination of the lease and the waiving of part of the rates arrears herself. She would then also have to negotiate terms for settlement of the PAYE liability and the liabilities to the trade creditors.

At this stage she had consulted an insolvency practitioner. She needed professional advice to explain what risks she was running and how best to minimise them.

It would have been safer to wait for someone to petition for the organisation's compulsory liquidation. However, Sarah wanted the business that she had loved and worked her heart out for to finish as tidily as possible, and with the best possible deal for everyone who was owed money.

If she had to drop the informal arrangement because she was not able to resolve the problems, she could have caused herself trouble and have left the position worse than if she had done nothing.

In the event, after a lot of hard work and considerable worry, the goodwill generated for this community business over the years, good relations with the local authority and good connections with other businesses who would pay a reasonable price for the assets gave this story a happy ending.

I am not sure whether Sarah would knowingly want to put herself through this again, though!

CHAPTER 3

GOING CONCERN STATUS: AN ACCOUNTANCY PERSPECTIVE

BY PESH FRAMJEE

This chapter discusses issues of relevance to both auditors and the charity's management when considering the question of going concern. It covers aspects of the accounting standards and best practice that must be borne in mind with regard to financial reporting. It discusses issues which impact on the going concern status such as the treatment of commitments, liabilities, post balance sheet events, balance sheet values. It also highlights particular areas of potential liability, such as tax, trading company and branch considerations, which may be overlooked when preparing accounts and other management reports.

Accounting standards

The year end accounts are often used to ascertain the financial position of the charity. They may not always be the best indicator of the charity's financial health, but they are certainly a relevant consideration. To understand how and to what extent accounts reflect the financial position and highlight the going concern status a brief discussion of some accounting standards and accounting practice is appropriate.

Accounts should be produced in a manner that meets certain standards. Statements of Standard Accounting Practice (SSAPs) and more recently issued Financial Reporting Standards (FRSs) are together seen as being authoritative statements on accounting practice. They aim to narrow the areas of difference and variety in the accounting treatments of the matters with which they deal and therefore to ensure that accounts are prepared on a broadly similar basis. They are applicable to all financial statements which are intended to give a true and fair view of the organisation's state of affairs at the balance sheet date and of income and expenditure for the financial period ending on that date. Compliance with accounting standards will normally be required if financial statements are to give a true and fair view.

Going concern status

SSAP2, which was issued in 1971, is probably the most fundamental accounting standard since its principles underpin most financial reporting practice in the UK. The statement deals with the disclosure of accounting policies and it discusses four fundamental accounting concepts, including the 'going concern' concept. Going concern is defined as being the understanding 'that the enterprise will continue in operational existence for the foreseeable future. This means in particular that the profit and loss account and balance sheet assume no intention or necessity to liquidate or curtail significantly the scale of operation'.

If activities were to be curtailed or assets were to be realised, this might create further losses resulting from forced sales, redundancy costs and so on. These are not usually taken into account when preparing accounts on a going concern basis unless it is probable that such losses are likely to arise in the foreseeable future.

The foreseeable future is deemed to be at least the period to the next balance sheet date. It should extend beyond that date to the extent that the trustees are aware of circumstances which could materially affect the viability of the organisation to keep going and hence cast doubts about the validity of using the going concern basis to prepare the accounts.

Concerns or doubts about the ability of the charity to remain a going concern do not automatically mean that the charity is insolvent. However, it is important to recognise that there may be an impact on the charity's solvency if doubts on going concern are disclosed. Where the trustees are unable to satisfy themselves that the organisation is going concern, they should consider taking professional advice. Where there is a question over the appropriateness of using the going concern basis in preparing accounts there may be other ramifications. For example, some donors may decide not to fund the organisation.

Contingencies

SSAP 18, published in August 1980, covers accounting for contingencies. The term contingency is applied to conditions which exist at the balance sheet date, where the outcome would be confirmed only on the occurrence or non-occurrence of one or more uncertain events. Examples of contingent liabilities could be a grant that has to be repaid for non-performance of the funder's conditions or the negative outcome of pending litigation.

It is important to distinguish between normal uncertainties and contingencies. For example, uncertainties connected with accounting estimates such as the life of a fixed assets, the net realisable value of stocks and the valuation of foreign currency balances are not contingencies. These are normal areas of uncertainty which are not usually referred to or amended in the accounts.

Contingencies should be reflected in the accounts according to the likelihood of their expected outcome. Material contingent losses should be accrued in financial statements where it is probable that a future event will confirm a loss which can be estimated with reasonable accuracy at the date on which the financial statements are approved by the trustees. Therefore, if it is probable that a contingent liability will materialise, then it should be accounted for, in other cases disclosure only may be appropriate.

The charity must consider carefully its exposure to contingent liabilities. It may be possible to use the benefit of hindsight based on past experience of matters such as legal proceedings and guarantees actually resulting in a liability. However, consideration is also necessary of contingencies in the future which may not have occurred in the past.

For instance, it will be necessary to review the terms of grants or assets bestowed to see whether there are any circumstances where they might have to be returned. Fundraisers or others may negotiate gifts of assets, grants, etc., which may have stringent conditions attached requiring their return or repayment if they cease to be used for a particular purpose. Such information is not always passed by the fundraiser to the finance department who prepare accounts, budgets and forecasts. As a result no proper assessment is made of the 'downside risk' facing the charity when making plans for the future and this can have unfortunate consequences.

Post balance sheet events

In addition to contingent liabilities that may occur in the future it is important to consider events that have actually occurred between the date of the balance sheet and the date on which the accounts are approved. Events arising after the balance sheet date need to be reflected in the accounts, if they provide additional evidence of conditions that existed at the balance sheet date and materially affect the amounts to be included.

Post balance sheet events are defined in SSAP17 as those events, both favourable and unfavourable, which occur between the balance sheet and the date on which the financial statements are approved by the board. The definition incorporates all events occurring between those dates irrespective of whether they existed at the balance sheet date. A distinction has to be made between those events that require 'adjusting' and those which are 'non adjusting'.

Adjusting events

Adjusting events are events which provide additional evidence relating to conditions which existed at the balance sheet date. These will require changes to the figures to be included in financial statements. For example, it is usual practice to accrue recoverable tax on deeds of covenant. However, if it was discovered after the end of the year that the covenantors could not be contacted to sign the necessary tax documentation, it would be wrong to include the reclaimable tax as a debtor in the accounts. Similarly, a change in taxation rates applicable to periods before the balance sheet would also be an adjusting event. These amounts should be adjusted, and as a result the balance sheet and solvency position might need to be reassessed.

Non-adjusting events

Non-adjusting events arise after the balance sheet date and concern conditions which did not exist at that time. Consequently, they do not require changes to the figures in the accounts but may however be material and important enough to the future financial that disclosures are required by way of note to the accounts to ensure that the accounts are not misleading.

For example, the charity's fixed assets may have been destroyed after the balance sheet date due to a fire or flood. This will of course require disclosure but no adjustment to the balance sheet since at the balance sheet date those fixed assets actually existed. Of course, although they do not affect the balance sheet, the impact of such an event on the going concern basis must be considered. If the charity is not properly insured, then the loss of significant assets would affect the view as to whether it could continue to operate into the foreseeable future.

Other considerations

There can be many grey areas in deciding whether an event is adjusting or non-adjusting. While SSAP17 states that the disposal of fixed assets after the balance sheet date is generally a non-adjusting event, it may be that the very large loss resulting from a disposal made after the balance sheet date could indicate that at that date a provision should have been made for a permanent diminution in value. In this case it would be correct practice to adjust the net book value at the balance sheet date.

Events occurring after the balance sheet date even if they are non-adjusting (for example, the deterioration in the level of appeal income, donations received, etc.), may indicate a need to reconsider whether it is still appropriate to use the going concern concept in the preparation of financial statements. Consequently, events of this nature even though occurring after the balance sheet date may need to be treated as adjusting events. Although they may not directly affect the figures they may cause an 'adjustment' to the view about going concern and therefore the basis of including figures in the accounts.

Statement of recommended practice

The original Statement of Recommended Practice on Accounting by Charities (SORP 2) was published in May 1988.

It is currently being revised under the auspices of the Charity Commission. It is expected that the new accounting regulations to be stipulated under the Charities Act 1993 will in the main endorse the new SORP. Although the objectives of charity accounting remain unchanged, experience has shown that the guidelines provided by the original SORP needed to be strengthened and clarified in certain areas. The thrust of the changes stems from a desire for greater accountability over all the resources entrusted to a charity and an intention to ensure that charity accounting follows the important requirements of trust law. The SORP makes a number of recommendations which merit discussion when considering the going concern and solvency position of a charity.

The bottom line

With most commercial organisations the 'bottom line' profit for the year is vitally significant. It is used as a measure of performance and evaluates the results for the period. In a standard profit and loss account, revenue and costs are matched since there is a strong relationship between them. For example, sales are matched with costs of sales associated overhead costs. These usually all relate to the same period and often to the same activities. In essence they are inter-dependent upon each other.

Charities are often not in the business of directly matching income and expenditure. Except where they enter into exchange contracts and make a charge for the provision of goods and services, the flow of income, be it from fundraising or investments, is not usually connected to the amount or timing of expenditure. For example, a charity may receive large amounts of money in the last few months of the year by way of an appeal or windfall legacy. The expenditure funded by this money may not be incurred until later accounting periods. Therefore, in the first year the accounts would show a very large surplus with a deficit in subsequent years if there had not been a commensurate increase in income for these years.

A traditional income and expenditure account with its distinction between revenue and capital does not fully explain a charity's activities. In some years the charity may use its general income to support capital expenditure, and the accounts might show that it has a surplus when it has in fact spent the money on fixed assets – which may be as important to its mission as is the revenue expenditure which appears in the income and expenditure account. Such a charity, although showing large surpluses on its income and expenditure account, may in fact be in a position where it is unable to sustain its activities in to the future since the resources of the charity are already tied up.

The SORP proposes a new primary statement called the Statement of Financial Activities (SOFA). This recognises that charities do not generally have any one single indicator of performance comparable to a business enterprise's bottom line, and that it is perhaps more important to consider the changes in the nature and as well as the amounts of the net resources of the charity. For example, a charity may purchase a property and net assets shown on the balance sheet will remain the same. The surplus for the year will also be unaffected but quite clearly the liquidity of the charity will be effected.

This is an important consideration since, although capital expenditure is not seen as a reduction in net resources, it is an all important change in the nature of those resources. Consideration has to be given as to how the charity has changed its resources, how it would be able to finance its future expenditure, commitments and plans, how the donor imposed restrictions on its resources will affect it, and how its capital spending will effect its liquidity and its ability to provide services.

Fund accounting

Trust law places constraints on how funds may be expended. These constraints are in the main based on donor imposed restrictions and this makes it important that due consideration is given to what the increase or decrease in net resources actually represents. A charity may, for example, maintain the level of its net resources only because it received income earmarked for a particular purpose (restricted income), which compensated for and masked a significant decrease in its general income. Thus although it apparently has a healthy position, it may in fact be running into difficulties.

Donor imposed restrictions often affect the types and levels of service the charity can deliver. Consequently, the information about the change in the nature of the net assets is most useful in assessing a charity's ability to respond to short term needs or provide higher levels of service. An analysis, as recommended by the SORP would be vital to be able to identify what services and activities the charity could continue to carry out, and this would be far more important than merely looking at a surplus or deficit on total revenue income and expenditure for the year. Therefore, the SORP recommends that the resources of a charity should be grouped according to the restrictions on their use as follows:

- **Unrestricted funds** – being funds available for general use and including those that have been designated for a particular purpose by the trustees of a charity. (The use of designated funds which can always be re-designated is a very important tool in ensuring that amounts which have been in some way committed without incurring an accounting liability are properly identified).

- **Temporarily restricted funds** – being income funds which are restricted for particular purposes either by the wishes of the donor or by the nature of the appeal;

- **Other restricted funds** – for example permanent endowments. These are usually sacrosanct and can not be expended without clearance from the donor of the Commissioners.

It is also important to consider how the funds are represented. For example, it makes no sense for restricted funds, which are required for a specified purpose in the short term, being invested in assets which can only be realised in the long term. This may seem a very simple concept but its surprising how many charities find themselves in the quandary of having invested their restricted funds in assets such as property or long term deposits which cannot be converted into cash when the funds are needed.

Expenditure

An important question when looking at the solvency of the charity is when and how it recognises a liability and reports it as expenditure. With commercial transactions expenditure is usually treated as not being incurred until consideration for the expenditure has passed – in other words, until something is received in exchange for the expenditure. However, in the case of charitable expenditure and grants relating directly to charitable activities, an exchange may not be involved. This exacerbates the problem, since it is not possible to match expenditure with the receipts of goods or services.

The original SORP was extremely prescriptive, and required that in such cases the expenditure should be accounted for when payment became due and not when it was committed. This created many problems and created the impression that some charities were 'far more solvent' than they were, since they were not recognising the liability of future commitments.

Recognising that this caused problems the exposure draft of the revised SORP considers that the issue is whether the grant payable or the expenditure is a legally enforceable obligation that could not be avoided. The recommendation was, if it is legally enforceable then it must be recorded in full and recognised as a liability immediately even if it is payable over a period of years. This is not an ideal solution but an attempt to try and achieve uniform implementation and a compromise solution. Nevertheless, it is clear that other important issues have to be considered regarding obligations and commitments when assessing the going concern position.

Obligations and commitments

A charity may make a promise to give. The dictionary definition of a promise is 'an assurance that one will do or not do something or will give or procure something'. Usually a promise means value, rights and obligations. The recipient has the right to receive something and the promisor has the obligation to give something.

Not all obligations are legally binding and their outcomes could be affected by future and uncertain events where there are intrinsic uncertainties about passing and receiving the benefit promised. For example, a charity may promise to support a three year project, but it may state that future payments were conditional on reviews of the work being carried out or on the funding being available. Future payments may in fact never be made, and there may be no method of enforcing that they are made. Although failure to make promised payments may be rare, many advocate that conditional promises to give should be recognised only when the conditional promise becomes unconditional and so creates an unavoidable obligation.

There is more to consider than whether there is a legally enforceable liability. Many liabilities rest on equitable or constructive obligations, and these are commonly paid in the same way as legally binding contracts. Although they lack the legal sanction, they are often felt to be binding on charity trustees, primarily because of social or moral criteria. Such equitable obligations stemming from ethical or moral constraints, rather than from accounting rules or legal provisions, are regarded and met in the same way as legal liabilities, perhaps they should also be accounted for in the same way.

Recognising a liability

A liability is a claim against the charity which:

- is expected to be settled by the charity parting with assets or in some way losing an economic benefit, and
- results from past transactions or events, and
- embodies a present duty and responsibility to one or more other entities that entail settlement at a specified or determinable future date on the occurrence of a specified event or on demand, and which
- results from a duty or responsibility which obligates the entity leaving it little or no discretion to avoid settlement.

This may appear clear in theory but is often obscured in practice. For example, many grant making charities believe that if they commit themselves to pay a grant, over a period of years, they should treat it all as a liability and accrue in full the amount that has been committed at the outset. Others would only account for the amounts when they fall due. Grants payable are accounted for in a myriad of different ways and this situation causes a lot of confusion in comparisons.

For example, a charity may agree to fund a researcher at £40,000 per year for three years. Some would accrue the whole £120,000 in the first year, whilst others would follow the original SORP and charge £40,000 in each of the three years. Another charity might itself directly employ the researcher at a salary of £40,000 and would only charge the year's expenditure as part of salary costs, even where the employment was for a fixed three year contact. Looking at the accounts to determine outstanding liabilities is not often sufficient. A careful evaluation of commitments at any point in time is needed.

The whole debate is fraught with anomalies. While some charities are keen to charge such commitments as expenditure in the current year, others are concerned that if they accrue in full for all future commitments they would show a negative balance sheet and thus appear to be insolvent. These charities stress that they are making these future commitments on the basis of future income streams. So to some extent there is a complementary asset to the liability, which may even be mirror images of each other.

Identifying the liability may lead to and require the identification of a corresponding asset. For example, a charity may have entered into a commitment to provide for the maintenance and education of children overseas. This expenditure may be funded by income from sponsors. In such cases, where future commitments are to be funded from future income streams it may not be appropriate to account for the liability and also to account for the future income; but it is vital to consider whether the likelihood of receiving the income it equal to the likelihood of having to make the payment.

In all cases it is important to consider the nature of any commitment. There may be a binding commitment by the charity to a third party who would receive the grant in the normal course of time. Alternatively, the payment may hinge on some eventuality or contingency – in effect a conditional grant. It is for this reason that budgets, forecasts and management accounts may be different to the statutory accounts, since the internal accounting must consider the impact of future commitments even though these may not be of the nature that are usually incorporated into year-end accounts.

Balance sheet asset values

The issue of what a balance sheet is meant to represent is one that has been argued at length. In April 1993 the Accounting Standards Board (ASB) produced a discussion paper on 'The role of valuation in financial reporting', it addresses what the ASB chairman has described as the `crunch issue' in British accounting. The problem stems from the fact that at present there is no consistency in valuation practice. In particular, assets may be included in the balance sheet at amounts representing current valuations, at earlier valuations or at historical cost. In the ASB's view this is unsatisfactory, and they have identified three options available to rectify the situation.

The first option is to a return to pure historical cost accounting. This is seen as a retrograde step as it would remove from financial statements relevant information of value to the users. The second option is to move to a full current value system. This return to current cost accounting is regarded as unsuitable because of the difficulties in obtaining sufficient reliability without incurring prohibitive costs. The preferred option is to continue with the present modified historical cost system, but attempting to remove some of the anomalies which exist.

In essence, the paper proposes a step-by-step approach to removing the anomalies in the present modified historic cost system by focusing initially on those assets for which supplementary information on current values is already required and which are traded on a 'ready market'.

Tangible fixed assets

Fixed assets are normally included in the balance sheet at cost less depreciation. It is important to realise that this does not reflect the market value. For example, if a charity purchases a minibus for £20,000 and expects to use it for 5 years, it will depreciate it at the rate of 20% per annum. At the end of the first year the minibus will be shown on the balance sheet at a value £16,000. This may not be the market value, since the market value of the minibus is unlikely to reduce evenly. However, the preparation of accounts on a going concern basis would base the accounting on the policy of writing off the asset over its estimated useful life, taking into account any residual values.

In cases where there is a permanent diminution in the value of an asset, the value should be adjusted to take account for this. It is important to recognise that the market value and value in use may be different and that fixed assets are not normally revalued each time the market values fluctuate. However, where a going concern basis is no longer appropriate, all valuations will have to be reconsidered.

Investments

The exposure draft of the SORP, which was published a few weeks before the ASB's paper, moves in the same direction. It recommends that investments should be valued at market value. The original SORP 2 allowed the option of either valuing at historical cost or at market value.

The revised SORP includes investment properties as a sub-category within investments, and these must also be included at market value. An investment property is defined as an interest in land and/or building in respect of which construction work and development have been completed and which is held to produce a return of income and capital, any rental income being negotiated at arm's length. Recognising that there may be a problem with property which is partly occupied for the charity's purposes and partly rented, the SORP excludes property which is mainly occupied by the charity for its own purposes.

The concept of valuing investments at market value sounds like heresy to some accountants used to valuing at the lower of cost or market value, but there is a general move to value investments at market value in most financial reporting. When faced with the choice of historical cost or market value, market value was chosen as being appropriate, since it more properly reflects at that particular date the value of the investments.

To emphasise the point that market value is likely to change, the SORP requires a disclosure of the unrealised gain. This would be the difference between the historical cost and the market value of investment. It is important that trustees and others when considering the financial position of the charity recognise that the market value, whilst perhaps more appropriate than cost, does not necessarily reflect the value available to the charity if it wished to realise its investments at a later stage. Changes in market conditions and transaction costs may lead to a different sum being realised.

Stocks

SSAP 9 deals with the valuation of stocks and work in progress and states that these should be reported at the lower of cost and market value. Where charities hold significant stocks it is appropriate for them to periodically assess their holdings and see whether any provision needs to be made for obsolescence or for some other factor resulting in the stock possibly not realising the value it is being carried at. Since accounts are normally prepared on a going concern basis, there is no need to consider a 'forced' sale situation but it is a salutary warning that very often in a solvency crisis stocks will not recognise the value that they are normally held at.

Debtors

Debtors are usually included in the balance sheet at the value which the charity thinks they will be recovered. A constant review of the debtors is important to ascertain whether they are in fact correctly stated. In many cases this may require consideration of the solvency position of the debtors. It is important not to let debts run up or remain outstanding for too long, these become harder to pay! Charities that have made loans or advances to other charities should carefully consider whether there is a likelihood of the loan being recovered, and therefore whether it is appropriate to carry the debtor in the balance sheet at its full value.

Tax liabilities

Contrary to popular misconception charities *are* affected by tax legislation, but many charities do not consider the ramifications of tax adequately and to their horror find they are often faced with back tax liabilities which can completely alter their solvency position. The main problem areas are:

Tax reclaims

Recovery of tax from the Inland Revenue is subject to stringent rules. The Inland Revenue operates a 'pay now check later' policy. As a result, charities may have received a reclaim of income tax and subsequently, following an Inland Revenue audit visit, there is evidence of non-compliance with the rules and the tax reclaim is disallowed. In many cases charities have had to repay tax they have claimed on deeds of covenants or gift aid where there was inadequate or defective documentation. Alternatively, the charity might have provided something in exchange for the donation, and thus jeopardised the tax effectiveness of the 'gift'. The moral here is to know the rules and see that they are followed to the letter.

VAT

VAT is probably the tax that affects charities most, since they incur VAT on so much of their expenditure. Problems can arise when charities fail to charge VAT on supplies or where they fail to register for VAT. In these cases they may have to account for the VAT that has not and should have been charged and also incur penalties for their failure to register.

Another common situation is where the charity has over-claimed input VAT. Typically, this may be due to an over optimistic apportionment or because it has breached the *de minimis* thresholds for reclaiming all the input tax. Subsequently it will have to make repayments and may also face misdeclaration penalties.

The problem can often be exacerbated by a solvency crisis. For example, a charity may have claimed input tax on computers or other capital assets it has purchased. As a result of a solvency crisis it may have to cut back on its operations and accordingly there may be a change of use in the property or equipment. In such cases the capital goods scheme may come into play and the charity may have to repay the input VAT it has already claimed. Thus charities have to monitor for several years the use of property and computer equipment above a certain value on which they have reclaimed input VAT.

Employment taxes

A charity is subject to employment tax legislation as much as any other employer. There are no special exemptions for charity employees, and charities might find that they are not complying the requirements for deducting and accounting for income tax and national insurance.

Most charities have no difficulty in recognising their core of regular employees and making the appropriate tax and national insurance deductions from their salaries. However, charity work invariably attracts various other personnel whose relationship with the charity is less clearly defined – voluntary helpers, part-timers, casuals, holiday reliefs, freelancers and so on. Failure to correctly operate PAYE and submit the correct returns at the right time can leave the charity to foot the tax bill and possible penalties.

In calculating the tax due where deductions have not been made, the amount that has been paid out is treated as a net sum which is then grossed up to calculate the tax liability. This can be very costly and in some cases can affect the solvency of the charity. Accordingly, it is relevant to assess whether correct deductions have been made from all employed staff, and also whether tax on benefits to employees and travel and subsistence payments are being correctly treated.

Direct taxes

Section 505 of the Income and Corporation Taxes Act 1988 (ICTA '88) gives exemption from tax on most of the main sources of charity income.

It is important that this is not construed as a general exemption from tax. For example, the rules governing trading are restrictive, and a charity will generally be taxable on trading profits unless the trade is exercised as part of the primary purpose or is carried out by the beneficiaries.

Many of the traditional areas of charity income generation are often within the wide description of trade which is found in Section 832 of ICTA '88. If there is a form of quid pro quo relationship and the charity provides something in exchange for the income it receives then the trading rules may apply. A failure to understand and operate by the rules may result in significant back tax liabilities which may effect the solvency of the charity.

Trading subsidiaries

Many charities have recognised the need to set up trading subsidiaries. The question then arises as to how to finance the trading subsidiary. The trading company will usually require working capital which could be made available by any one of the following ways:

- borrowing from a commercial source
- borrowing from the charity
- the issue of share capital.

The Charity Commissioners have stated that if funds are needed to sustain or expand the activities of the trading company, they should normally be obtained from a commercial source. There are however many problems obtaining money from a commercial lender who will most certainly request and require a guarantee from the charity or from its trustees.

The charity must have the constitutional powers to give such a guarantee. As a general rule, it is a fundamental tenet of charity law that the charity should not give away its own assets except in the furtherance of its charitable purposes. The giving of a gratuitous guarantee of this nature could be tantamount to giving away assets if the guarantee was called. However, case law has shown that in certain cases the giving of such a guarantee will be within the powers of a corporate charity but this would only usually apply if the company on whose behalf the guarantee was given was a wholly owned subsidiary of the charity and was carrying out the objects of the charity. The first condition is not difficult to achieve, but the second may be a stumbling block.

There are many issues to be considered in the charity's relationship with its trading subsidiary.

Liabilities of the trading subsidiary

Not all trading companies are profitable. In fact, there have been cases where trading subsidiaries have collapsed owing considerable sums of money. The Charity Commissioners addressed this issue in their 1988 report which refers to the liquidation of Search 88 and Company Limited owing £700,000 and Sports Aid Limited owing between £2m and £3m. In both these cases the charity trustees and promoters followed sound and recommended advice in order to protect the assets of their charities.

In one of the cases, the creditors thought that they were dealing with a charity rather than an arm's length limited liability company. It is vital that it is made clear to those involved as to whether the transactions are with the charity or with its subsidiaries. Failed subsidiaries often leave the charity's trustees in dilemma. In order to avoid the adverse publicity which may arise and because of a perceived moral obligation to the creditors, they may wish to settle the liabilities of the trading subsidiary using the charity's assets. Such a course of action would normally be outside the trustees' powers.

When a subsidiary is making losses there might be a tendency to expect better times, and this can lead to large losses being run up over a period of time. It is also worth mentioning the possibility of the directors of a trading subsidiary being found guilty of wrongful trading under Section 214 of the Insolvency Act 1986. Directors are expected to conform to an objective standard of ability, and should be aware of the current position of the company. They should act with extreme caution where insolvency looms. Where there appears to be no reasonable prospect of avoiding liquidation, there is a need to take immediate steps to minimise the loss to creditors.

Similarly, the charity trustees may be personally liable if they continue to prop up a failing subsidiary by lending it charitable funds, as this would constitute a breach of trust. It is important that the charity trustees regularly consider any loans or investments they have made in trading subsidiaries. They must also consider carefully before they issue letters of comfort on behalf of trading subsidiaries or guarantee the loans or liabilities of trading subsidiaries.

Joint VAT registrations

It is sometimes expedient for the charity to have a joint VAT registration with its trading subsidiary. This arrangement can often mitigate the VAT burden for the charity and its subsidiary by allowing enhanced recovery of input VAT and dispensing with a need to charge VAT on inter-company transactions. However, the taking of such joint registration also means that all parties to the joint registration are liable for the VAT liabilities of each other. This is similar to the charity given a guarantee on behalf of the trading subsidiary which may result in the charity having to meet the VAT liability of the trading subsidiary.

Joint registration could perhaps be seen as acceptable where there is a definite financial benefit to the charity as a result of the joint registration. The trustees should take sound professional advice that it would be in the financial interest of the group to enter into joint VAT registration, and should also consider the probability of the trading subsidiary failing and the charity having to meet any VAT liability before entering into a joint registration. Any joint VAT registration must be in the interest of the charity, and should be reviewed regularly to ensure that the trustees are not exposing themselves unduly to the risk of having to meet the VAT liability of a failed trading subsidiary.

Branches

It is important that the charity carefully considers the impact of the activities of its branches on its own going concern status. The question of accounting and financial reporting for branches is one that has often been glossed over. To simplify the financial reporting and operational issues, there has been a tendency to treat branches as 'autonomous'. The question of whether a branch is autonomous or not is usually a matter of legal fact, and the attitude of branch members or of head office is not the deciding factor. It is of fundamental importance to ascertain whether the branches are part of the main charity or whether they are truly autonomous entities fully responsible for their own actions and any liabilities which may arise from them.

Usually if funds are raised or an activity is carried out in the name of the parent charity, then there is a presumption of involvement by the parent charity. There are many questions to consider. For example, who 'owns' funds held at a local branch. Particularly, what would happen if either the branch or the parent charity were to close or make some other call on the funds. The fact that the branch runs its own bank account is not the deciding factor.

All the issues discussed in this chapter of going concern status and liabilities apply equally to branches, and it is important to ascertain whether the liabilities of the branch automatically will become the liabilities of the parent. Trustees should attempt to ascertain the position should a legal action be taken against the branch, so that they know the possible impact on the parent charity. If there was a disaster at a branch fundraising event and proper insurance was not available, would it be the parent or the branch that was sued? In a recent case, branches had been historically treated as autonomous but wrongly so, and the parent charity was held liable for the claims of employees and other liabilities at a branch level.

Charities should carefully review their operating structures to establish whether the branches need to be reported on as part of the charity. Even where a decision may be taken that branches are not included in the parent charity's accounts perhaps on grounds of materiality, it is important to consider whether they are truly separate legal entities. It may also be worth considering whether the relationship between the parent charity and its branches needs to be put on a more explicit footing – perhaps making the branches autonomous and responsible for their own affairs, but requiring certain standards of values, quality and operation in return for using the parent charity's name and logo.

Similar considerations apply at a branch level. The branch may hold funds on special trusts for the charity and such funds received for the charity may not be available to meet liabilities at a branch level. There are no simple answers. It is important to consider the particular circumstances, the constitutional position of the charity and its branches, and any agreements between them.

The contract culture

Many charities are firmly enmeshed in the contract culture, while others are tentatively entering it. Over the past few years, there has been a shift from general grant aid to legally enforceable contracts and service agreements, with all the attendant risk and exposure for the charity. In effect, the charity is undertaking to provide a service at a stated level and of a specified quality in exchange for a fee or a charge. It is therefore vitally important that the charity ensures that it has the resources to provide that service, and that the fee it is charging at least covers the costs it will be incurring.

For example, a charity may have budgeted in its contract to provide residential care for ten individuals at a certain fixed price per individual. The costing may have been based upon the assumption of full occupancy. But if full occupancy is not achieved, the fixed costs will not be fully covered as budgeted and the charity may find it is running at a loss. In some cases it may be able to obtain a 'top up' payment, but in many cases this will not be possible and the charity will be depleting its reserves.

This underlines the importance of getting the costing right from the outset. The aim should be to cover not just direct costs but also deprecation, a reasonable allocation of overheads, any research and development expenditure, and all other costs incurred in maintaining a successful operation.

Charities should be wary about taking on contracts and entering into joint ventures without considering their implications. There are other areas to consider. The Trade Union Reform and Employment Rights Act 1993 makes important amendments to the Transfer of Undertaking (Protection of Employment) Regulations 1991. Consequently, there may be continuing employment rights when an undertaking is transferred to a new employer, for example if one organisation merges with another or takes over a grant from another. It is now clear that the regulations apply to voluntary non-profit organisations, and in many cases employers' contracts of employment and attendant liabilities will transfer to the new organisation. Failure to consider this liability could create a problem when the contract comes to an end and alternative work can not be found for the employees.

Levels of reserves

It is important for a charity to have some reserves to cater for lean times. A number of charities having followed what seemed to be a laudable intention of spending all their income on their charitable purposes find that in times of need there is no buffer. In some cases they have had to make cut backs, retrench staff and dramatically failed their beneficiaries because they did not have sufficient levels of reserves to sustain their activities. Sometimes, this is only a temporary crisis and increased income and activity levels in the future may require re-employment of new staff. Clearly, it makes sense to have a safety net.

There are many factors to be considered when deciding what level of reserves is appropriate. One of the criteria would be whether the nature of expenditure is fixed or variable and how it compares with the volatility of income. The ability of the charity to change gear must also be considered. For example, if there is a drop in income, is it possible for there to be a commensurate saving in expenditure. Charities could perform a form of 'sensitivity analysis' and consider what would happen if there was a 5-10% decrease in income or an increase in costs. The question to ask is, is there a buffer to carry them through while new income is generated or costs are reduced. The question of commitments and obligations to beneficiaries and staff cannot be overstressed. Past performance and trends must also be considered.

When deciding on a 'safe' level of reserves, the nature of the reserves themselves is important. How liquid are they? What is the investment medium and what is the yield? If the realisable value of the reserves can change significantly and differ from book values, then the implications of this will need to be considered.

The issue of reserves is very important. Each charity will have to decide on its own reserves policy, bearing in mind its own particular circumstances and the possible impact on fundraising and morale within the charity if seemingly high cash balances or investments are not adequately explained.

Governance and stewardship

The Cadbury Committee which reported on corporate governance in December 1992 made many recommendations for commercial business which have strong parallels in the voluntary sector. One of the requirements of the Cadbury Committee's code was that directors (in the context of charities, this would be the charity trustees) should state in their annual report whether or not the entity is a going concern, with supporting assumptions given as necessary and that the auditors should report on this statement. This recommendation has now been incorporated into an auditing standard. In May 1993 a working group produced draft recommendations on how to comply with this requirement.

The working group's paper identifies the procedures available in determining that the going concern assumption is appropriate. It sets up criteria which should be applied in evaluating the results of the procedures and recommends the appropriate disclosure.

The paper suggests that procedures should be drawn up with an understanding of the critical factors which could effect the going concern status of the organisation. These factors will vary according to the type of charity and also over time. Many of the procedures suggested by the paper have been covered by Adrian Randall in *Chapter 4*. Charities which operate sound financial management and control systems will in effect already be following these procedures. Three areas which are important in the context of monitoring the financial stability are discussed below.

Management information

Management information is crucial in a charity. Important decisions are taken by Trustees, members of council, committees and senior paid executives. Their time is precious. Consequently, the importance of sound, effective management information systems cannot be emphasised. This requires the integration and interpretation of relevant non-financial operational information with accounting data to provide information that can be used effectively. Management information is more than just management accounting and budgeting.

Effective decision-making requires effective information. To be able to evaluate the impact of a charity's past actions and to plan for and assess the implications of its future activities it is vital that proper and sufficient information is available.

At the same time too much management information is counterproductive. The information should concentrate on areas where control can be exercised and on those factors which are critical for the success of the organisation. These could include:

- **Resource budgets and forecasts:** to include financial and other important resources such as time and people. For example, a charity may be dependant on volunteer support and if this is curtailed the operating capacity and financial viability may be dramatically affected.

- **Ongoing performance:** which should be monitored so that any necessary action can be taken. This may require an analysis of the critical success factors that a charity needs to concentrate on to succeed. The reports should measure achievements in these areas.

- **Donors and other funders:** may need to be constantly reviewed to see if the charity is meeting their effectiveness criteria. If it is not then these important stakeholders may take their support elsewhere.

- **Beneficiaries:** the needs of the beneficiaries and clients of the charity should be constantly reviewed. The charity must set its strategies in furtherance of its objectives. It will need periodically to assess and report on how well it is meeting its goals and the needs of the different classes of its clients and beneficiaries.

- **Key ratios and exception reports:** these are often useful to identify departures from the expected norms. Thus if everything is 'ticking over' as expected, no detailed report is required. Parameters for variances must be set so that important variances can be identified, investigated and actioned.

In the process of assisting with designing practical and user-friendly information systems it is important to consider:

- exactly what management information is required
- who needs it and why they need it
- how it will be prepared and by whom
- if it can be obtained as a by-product of another process
- whether the cost of having the information is commensurate with the benefit from using it
- if the needs of different users can be catered for by tailoring different reports
- for how long information should be stored, and when historic information should be deleted or archived.

Budgeting

Budgeting and planning and the correct allocation of income and expenditure is of crucial importance especially where it is necessary to match variable income against fixed commitments. The budgetary control process is a must to ensure a match between short-term activities and longer-term strategy. Good budgeting is therefore required to co-ordinate operations, control subsequent expenditure and, by setting targets, provide the means to motivate.

All managers and not just the financial staff should be involved in the budget setting process. This is often done by considering the previous budget and adding inflation to this. This form of incremental budgeting may be simple to do and appropriate in many circumstances, but it suffers from drawbacks particularly where substantial changes are taking place. Even when an incremental budgeting process is used, it is still useful periodically to review the organisation's activities and prepare the budget from first principles. Zero based budgeting of this nature, whilst time consuming, will be essential where there have changes in the organisation's direction, activity level or approach.

It is vital that charities have the actual resources available when they are needed. These can be staff skills and time, as well as money. Income will be required to meet expenditure when it falls due. Consequently, the need for good income forecasting and income appraisal cannot be overemphasised. In particular, there should be internal systems to monitor carefully and on a regular basis income flows against forecast, and actual expenditure against planned expenditure. These can then be used to generate forecasts for the year, a form of flexed budget based on actuals to date and estimates for future periods.

The auditors/trustees duties and responsibilities

In May 1993, the Auditing Practice Board published its first statement of auditing standards SAS 600 on the auditors' report on financial statements. This applies to accounting periods ending on or after 30 September 1993 and changes the form of auditors' reports where there are doubts about the appropriateness of the going concern basis. Auditors will now explain within the audit report the respective responsibilities of the trustees and auditors. The statement will state that the trustees are responsible for the preparation of the financial statements and there will be a statement from the trustees in their report that the accounts have been prepared on a going concern basis (unless this basis is inappropriate.)

SAS 600 has changed the form of audit reports particularly where there are doubts about the appropriateness of the going concern. If there are substantial doubts about the appropriateness of the going concern basis this is a fundamental uncertainty. The fundamental uncertainty therefore needs to be properly disclosed in the financial statements and if it is not so properly disclosed then it is a matter for qualification in the audit report. However, if the trustees have made proper disclosure in the accounts then the basis of the auditors' opinion need only include an explanatory paragraph referring to the uncertainty while making it clear that the explanation does not amount to a qualification.

Obtaining outside help

Charities may on occasion need to seek professional advice. They should use professional advisors who understand the peculiarities of the voluntary sector. Close contact and good rapport is essential. The charity should discuss with their professional advisers their future plans and any problem areas they may foresee. In many cases an independent review of ideas and plans will be helpful, and the adviser might play 'devil's advocate' to ensure full consideration of the potential 'down side' of new schemes and projects. At the same time an experienced adviser can assist the charity find answers to difficult operational issues.

Sometimes a charity's own management may be too closely involved with the cause or are 'bogged down' with the difficult problem. In some cases this may result in them missing the wood for the trees. For example, a charity was burdened with heavy borrowing at high interest rates. The charity was finding it difficult to meet its repayments and the interest. The charity also had endowed capital funds which had always been treated as sacrosanct. External advisers questioned this assumption and identified the potential of using capital funds to reduce borrowings, and a scheme was agreed with the Charity Commissioners to do this. By reducing its external debt and agreeing a schedule of recoupment/reinstatement of capital, the charity was able to pull itself out of a vicious spiral of ever-increasing debt.

Charity managers should also consult widely with others working in the voluntary sector to ensure that they are aware of any political, economic and social trends which might impact on their own organisation. An early recognition of threats (and any opportunities) which could significantly affect the organisation and its work will allow charities to plan ahead and ensure that their organisation remains a going concern.

CHAPTER 4:

MANAGING YOUR SOLVENCY: THE FINANCIAL ADMINISTRATOR'S PERSPECTIVE

BY ADRIAN RANDALL

It is important to understand clearly what one is looking at in relation to *insolvency* or *going concern* as it affects a charity or other voluntary organisation.

Many organisations are operating close to that thin dividing line between these two positions. Some may well even be technically insolvent as defined by a practising accountant, who may well interpret the situation somewhat differently from the financial administrator – for when that next donation, subsidy, sponsorship, grant, legacy or whatever cheque arrives, suddenly the organisation appears to be solvent again.

However, it is far better to be sensible about this, and to follow fundamental accounting concepts when looking at solvency. At all times prudence should play a part in computing the assets and more importantly the liabilities of the organisation.

A financial administrator should at all times be aware of problems that are likely to arise before they do arise.

What does 'going concern' mean?

'Going concern' is the ability to continue in operation *for the foreseeable future*, even if this means curtailing some of the charity's operations, *provided that* the primary purpose can be continued.

This means particularly that the charity has no intention to liquidate or reduce significantly the state of its operation, nor is this necessary. Thus, the primary purpose is maintained and will go on being pursued.

The 'foreseeable future' may well vary from charity to charity, but it is usually defined to include at least that period up to the next balance sheet date. Defining the *de minimis* period as being to the next balance sheet date is practical, as it recognises that the usual basis for forecasting budgets is by financial years. However, the overriding principle is that the trustees should take into account all the evidence available to them which could affect the going concern status of the charity. They will be advised by the financial administrator (or finance director) who is in day-to-day touch with the finances of the organisation in consultation with the chief executive, where appropriate, on matters that concern the charity overall.

It is worth remembering that doubts about going concern basis do not automatically equal insolvency. Even where the going concern status is in doubt, it is possible to continue for the time being and to turn round the situation. An organisation will not be considered a going concern if it intends to curtail the extent of its operations so severely that it would cease to perform its principal activities.

Procedures to establish financial status

There are many factors which the financial administrator should consider in deciding whether or not the organisation is a going concern. These would include the broad headings of:

- quantitative factors
- qualitative factors
- internal factors and
- external factors.

In any organisation the financial administrator will be the best placed to know the critical factors which could and will affect the going concern status of their particular organisation. These critical factors will vary from one type of charity to another, and could also vary from one organisation to another within any particular group. For example, one charity may well have an over-dependence on one particular donor, whilst another charity operating in the same field may well have a wide spread of donors but a lease on a property imposing considerable obligations on it. Critical factors can of course change over time.

The procedures to establish an organisation's financial status are an important management tool as a matter of routine. Even where the organisation appears healthy, a regular scrutiny can help show trends at an early stage when it is still possible to do something. Where the organisation is near the brink of financial unviability, it is particularly important to keep a close and frequent scrutiny of the financial position.

Quantitative factors

Forecasts and budgets

Forecasting and budgeting are very long established techniques in management accounting, and therefore in the operation of any well run business, whether commercially or not for profit. Unfortunately sometimes these techniques are used in a purely mechanical way without a full consideration being taken of the key assumptions and the consequences of the variances from budget in the management accounts. However, where the critical assumptions are challenged and tested and logical deductions are made from the variance analysis, refined budgets and forecasts can become powerful predictive techniques. It is essential therefore that the organisation prepares monthly budgets and cash flow forecasts to cover the period up to the next balance sheet date as an absolute minimum. Ideally, of course, these budgets and forecasts should be prepared on a rolling basis for the next twelve months ahead (or longer).

Testing the assumptions

The treasurer and the trustees and also the chief executive should confirm that in drawing up the budgets and forecasts:

- that the assumptions used are consistent with past performance
- the income projections are realistic
- the assumptions are based on working capital requirements that are sensible
- the basis of payment terms with creditors is attainable.

It is of course essential to determine which assumptions are critical to the continuing operation of the organisation, and then to test these thoroughly. The financial administrator should consider whether forecasts adequately provide for changes in costs and take sufficient account of the depreciation, maintenance and replacement costs of fixed assets. Many organisations have seasonal fluctuations in income and expenditure which will need to be looked at when preparing budgets and forecasts. The key assumptions may well be sensitive to different levels of activity, and this needs to be tested.

Disclosure of the critical assumptions relating to the income and expenditure projections and to the future of the organisation is undoubtedly a key element in a proper understanding of the going concern statement, whether these assumptions are appended to that statement or set out elsewhere in the annual report and accounts.

While what happened in the past is never a fully accurate guide to what will happen in the future, the accuracy of past forecasts, over say the last three years, should be looked at. Any significant variances should be analysed and documented, and the financial administrator should consider whether the current forecast needs revising to avoid the same underlying tendencies and errors.

Monitoring performance

Having put considerable effort into drawing up accurate budgets and forecasts, it is important to monitor your actual performance on an ongoing basis. It will always be necessary to have a contingency plan to cope with temporary shortfalls. What is more important is to be able to identify what are more than temporary shortfalls and take remedial action. *Trend analysis* is a useful mechanism for doing this.

Regular health checks of your financial situation are vital to determine your current status and ongoing potential. This is where *liability management* comes into play.

Looking at cash flow

The financial administrator should ensure that at any point in time the financial plans show an adequate matching of known cash outflows with projected cash inflows. For many organisations, expenditure is far easier to forecast than income, so it is important that expenditure should include all known liabilities, such as payments to creditors, to ensure that everything is taken into account.

Assessing liability

The financial administrator should produce a schedule of all known liabilities, together with the dates on which the payments fall due, and this schedule should extend beyond the next balance sheet date. It is important to include not only actual liabilities, but also an assessment of all *potential* liabilities, those liabilities *contingent* upon certain activities taking place.

Identifying substantial outflows

Particular attention should be given to those periods when large payments are due and there are no anticipated inflows of funds to match them. Such situations can cause temporary embarrassment and need to be planned for. There are always liabilities that can be postponed, but certain types of payment such as VAT and PAYE must be made on their due dates. Where the projections show outflows are not matched by inflows, the financial administrator will have to consider how funds can be raised (or borrowed, in anticipation of a later inflow), and whether the money can be in place to cover the payments as they fall due. Some organisations have the constitutional power to borrow. However, many will not have this facility available, either because their governing instrument does not allow it or because the lending institutions do not see them as a sufficiently good risk.

Hidden liabilities

It is important in drawing up the list of contingent liabilities to take account of any commitments which, in accountants language, may be 'off balance sheet'. An example of this is where the organisation has acquired assets on operating leases. These will not be included as a capital item in the balance sheet, but there is a commitment to make all future payments due under the terms of the lease.

The funding of present and future liabilities needs to be very carefully assessed, particularly in risky areas. It is important to assess the financial viability of those who are funding the organisation, those who are purchasing or paying for its services and other trading partners and, where there is cause for concern, to have strategies to deal with the risks involved.

Borrowing capability

Any borrowing facilities that are available to the organisation should be compared with the cash flow forecast to see if they are adequate for the period up to the next balance sheet as an absolute minimum. If they are not, then either more money will have to be raised or the borrowing facilities increased. The financial administrator should ascertain as far as it is possible that there are no actual or anticipated:

• cash flow deficits

• arrears of interest

• breaches of borrowing restrictions (where appropriate).

If there is a borrowing facility, then there is the responsibility to manage it properly. At all times it is essential that any potential deficits, arrears or breaches be discussed with the lenders to alert them to potential problems and to determine what action is appropriate, and then to ensure that such action is taken.

Monitoring performance

At least monthly (depending on the size of the organisation), a comparison should be made between the monthly cash flow forecast (prepared previously) with the actual position. This is to ensure that everything is going more or less as planned, and that there are no major variances. It is not sufficient just to look at the bottom line. It may be that a major grant has been received some months earlier than forecast, which will significantly distort the position. Use should be made of *sensitivity analysis*, to look at the worst case scenario based on the assumptions used in forecast, and to think about what you should do in such an eventuality.

At all times when monitoring actual performance against budget/ forecast, it is important to take any remedial action as quickly as possible.

Exposure to contingent liabilities

The financial administrator should review from time to time the organisation's exposure to contingent liabilities. In doing this you need to consider not only liabilities experienced by the charity in the past which might recur in the future, such as legal proceedings, but also to consider potential new areas of liability such as the financial effects of the Charities Act 1993. A full analysis should be carried out of the exposure to contingent liabilities. As an example, where the organisation has been in receipt of grants for revenue or capital expenditure and there were conditions attaching to those grants, you should consider whether there has been or is likely to be a breach of those conditions such that a repayment is or will be due as a consequence. Grants received for a specific purpose cannot usually be utilised for any other purpose without the consent of the donor.

Qualitative factors

Qualitative factors are much harder to identify and evaluate than quantitative factors, but can also be used to assess the going concern basis of the organisation. Here we are dealing not so much with the numbers but with the relationships.

Assets

Looking at the assets of the organisation, you should ask about the physical state of those assets, whether they are new or old, well looked after or dilapidated etc. An audit of the physical state of assets of a charity is an essential ongoing activity.

Staff

Many organisations' greatest asset is their staff. In assessing going concern status, it is essential to determine factors such as turnover of staff, the general morale, the level of training, etc. The following questions should also be checked and answered:

- Are there appraisal systems in operation?
- What is the quality of work?
- How is it evaluated?

Relationships with funders

A close look should be taken at relationships with major funders, sponsors and stakeholders to ascertain the quality of the various sources of income. Is the organisation on good terms with its major funders? Have good personal working relationships been established? Does the organisation report back regularly and can it demonstrate an effective use of the funds? Is the organisation aware of the financial background and stability of its major funders, and are there any dangers looming?

Performance and quality of work

Often the funding is linked to the provision of a particular service, for example, a residential home for the elderly funded (wholly or partially) by a local authority. In cases like these, it is essential to ensure that the quality of work carried out by the organisation meets the required standards laid down by the funder, and that there is feedback on this topic to the funder. Even where there is no direct relationship between the grant and the service provided, the funder will still be interested to see that a high quality service is being delivered, and this can influence future funding decisions.

It is very difficult looking at qualitative factors alone to assess accurately the financial position, which is of course itself a quantitative judgement. Also, qualitative factors vary in significance from organisation to organisation. However it remains important when looking at the solvency and going concern status of an organisation to consider qualitative as well as quantitative factors because they can also contribute to the viability of the organisation and give a perspective on its financial health.

Internal and external factors

Using a business analogy, internal and external factors are best described as 'products and markets'. Many of the issues which could be included under this heading will have already been addressed in looking at quantitative and qualitative factors.

The operating environment

The financial administrator should have information about the most important aspects of the economic environment within which the organisation operates. You need to consider the size of the market place, your own organisation's particular strengths and weaknesses, your share of the market, and whether there are any economic, political or other factors which may create changes. Consideration should also be given to the standing of the organisation, how this has changed over time, and whether it is likely to change in the foreseeable future.

Image and accountability

You should consider whether the public image, behaviour and perceptions of the organisation are consistent with public expectation and fully meet the standards of accountability. Internally you will need to consider the adequacy of the accounting systems and to review the accuracy of these systems in providing adequate information and to see whether the systems themselves need updating. It is essential that performance measurement should be reviewed and acted upon in order to maintain the performance of the organisation as a whole.

The funding mix

You need to consider the mix of donors, whether the organisation's income is dependent on a limited number of these and whether there is a risk for example of losing any donors (particularly at short notice with little chance of replacement).

The pattern of support

You will need to look at the consistency of donation and membership income. Is this steady, or rising, or declining? Will present trends continue? Are fundraising costs reasonable? Have ways and means been sought to generate new sources of income at reasonable cost? You should carry out periodic reviews of your donors and must also consider the likelihood of finding alternative income sources where there appears to be a high risk of losing existing donors.

Other factors

There are many other factors which could affect a charity's going concern status. Examples might include:

- consistency of income
- stability of cost base
- recurring operating losses (trading subsidiaries)
- labour difficulties
- non-compliance with Charities Act 1993
- loss of key management
- adequacy of insurance cover.

Disclosures

Having carried out thoroughly the procedures to establish the financial status, as outlined above, you reach one of the following three conclusions:

- You will be satisfied that the organisation *is a going concern*, and that there is a reasonable expectation that it will continue into the foreseeable future, or

- You will be unable to satisfy yourself that the organisation is a going concern, on the basis that you are **not sure** about its viability for the foreseeable future, or

- You consider that the organisation is *not a going concern*, on the basis that you have no reasonable expectation that it will continue in the foreseeable future.

If you have reached the first conclusion then there is no problem for the organisation and it will be able to go on operating and it can issue accounts on the going concern basis with a suitable statement to that effect.

If you come to the second conclusion, the organisation will still be able to issue accounts and continue operating, but there must be a statement in those accounts drawing attention to the particular circumstances that are causing concern. The trustees or committee members will have to point out that they have not been able to satisfy themselves that the organisation is a going concern. In this case there must be an explanation of the material circumstances setting out the full reasons.

If you have come to the third conclusion, then it would certainly not be appropriate for the trustees to prepare accounts on a going concern basis. In these circumstances the trustees should take legal advice on the wording of the statement that they would have to issue explaining that the organisation is not or no longer a going concern. It would then be necessary to consider whether the organisation itself is insolvent and should be wound up.

If there is any cause for concern, then as financial administrator you should prepare a report for the senior management team and the trustees setting out the situation as you see it, with your conclusions and recommendations.

Summary

It is never going to be easy to identify in advance all the cases of worry of an 'insolvency or going concern' nature. Hindsight is marvellous! Many of the signs by which one could tell that a business is in trouble will unfortunately be useless when looking at charities and voluntary organisations because of their special nature.

There are many types of risks facing a charity or a voluntary organisation, and you should identify which risks are critical to your own organisation. For example, in the case of a third world charity operating overseas, the exposures to movements in foreign currency rates and political stability may be significant risks. For a grant-making research charity operating entirely in the UK, these factors will be of little or no importance at all. It is essential therefore, that you consider what risks you face, how these risks affect your charity and then decide how best to manage them.

Although knowledge of what has happened in the past is helpful, it cannot be used *in isolation* to predict the sensitivity of the organisation to future events. You should use your understanding of the organisation, its resources and the state of the markets in which it functions to determine those key factors which could affect its future.

The ability of the organisation to take effective action to alter the amounts and timing of cash inflows and outflows, to respond to unexpected needs or opportunities, and to take substantive action to redress any problem is of paramount importance. The watchword must be caution, and as the Charity Commission advises in their booklets for trustees, prudence should be uppermost.

CHAPTER 5

INSOLVENCY AND LIABILITY: THE TRUSTEE PERSPECTIVE

BY LINDSAY DRISCOLL

Responsibilities of trustees for the affairs of the charity

Charity trustees are defined by Section 97 of the Charities Act 1993 as the persons having the general control and management of the administration of a charity. They have legal responsibility for the conduct of the organisation. They have a number of far-reaching duties and responsibilities. These can be divided into legal, financial and management responsibilities. On the legal side they must act strictly in accordance with the charity's governing document (constitution) and take special account of the objects and powers and of any restrictions (e.g. regarding trading, investments, use of funds). The income and property of the charity must be applied for the purposes set out in the governing document and for no other purpose. They must also ensure that the organisation complies with the law. This includes charity law, trust law, company law, insolvency law, employment law, contract law and many other areas of law and individual statutes.

Acting prudently

Trustees are under a general duty to act reasonably and prudently in all matters relating to the charity. They should exercise the same degree of care in dealing with the administration of the charity as a prudent businessman or woman would exercise in managing his or her own affairs. It follows from this general rule that trustees are responsible to ensure prudent financial management for the organisation and must exercise overall control over its financial affairs. They must not undertake expenditures for which insufficient resources are available.

In respect of investments, a trustee has a higher duty and must act as a prudent businessman would if he were handling other people's monies and not his own. The governing document of the charity will usually set out the powers of investments, and modern charities often have very wide powers. If there is no express power, the trustees of unincorporated charities will be subject to the Trustee Investments Act 1961. All trustees must have regard to the need for diversification, must assess the suitability of investments (both the type of investment and the actual example) and must obtain and consider proper advice on these matters. They should also avoid speculative or risky investments.

The question of breach of trust can arise if loss occurs through negligent investment in a subsidiary trading company. The trustees can only invest in a trading subsidiary if this is authorised in the governing document. It would not be authorised under the Trustee Investment Act. They must also consider the profitability of the trading subsidiary as they should be able to demonstrate that the investment is not speculative. In the case of a loan to the trading subsidiary, this must be on a commercial basis so that the rate of interest payable, the terms of repayment and security must all be assessed on this basis. Another difficulty with investment in a trading subsidiary is that it is a non-qualifying expenditure for tax purposes.

Leases and contracts

Trustees must exercise particular care in taking on long-term obligations or liabilities where their funding is on a short-term basis. Leases are frequently a problem for charities. They are often faced with taking on a long-term obligation against short-term funding. It is often difficult to persuade a landlord to accept an early surrender of the lease or an assignment to another tenant where this is prohibited under the terms of the lease. Where a lease is assigned, the obligations and liabilities contained in the lease will still be a burden on the charity in the event of failure of the assignee – unless the landlord specifically agrees to release the trustees, which is a most unusual event.

Trustees should know the terms and conditions of all leases entered into (and this includes leases for equipment as well as for property). Steps can be taken to minimise the risk. In some cases a periodic tenancy (i.e. one with a very short notice period) would be appropriate. If possible, the lease should contain a right to assign without continuing liability on charity. A quarter or a half year's rent can be set aside as a reserve and kept on deposit against liabilities under the lease. It is important to realise that liability extends not only to payment of rent but also to dilapidations.

Other long-term contracts also present potential problems. Photocopier leasing agreements are a particular source of difficulty as termination of the contract before the end of its term often involves heavy financial penalties.

Financial management

Trustees have the general duty of protecting the charity's property and safeguarding the assets. This is a wide-ranging obligation. It includes proper investment of funds, good financial systems and controls (including financial reporting, frequency and content, budgeting, internal controls and audit), insurance protection and preservation of endowments. Care needs to be taken to determine the best structures and procedures for discharging this duty. It is sometimes appropriate to establish a sub-committee with a specific brief to monitor the charity's finances.

Commitments to donors

Trustees have responsibilities to meet their commitments to their donors and funders, to their employees, to third parties under contracts and to their beneficiaries. These commitments may be general or involve compliance with very specific terms and conditions. If a source of funding fails, trustees must endeavour to secure sufficient resources to meet commitments and ensure the continued operation of the charity.

Risk

The legal and financial responsibilities of charity trustees necessitate the adoption of a strategy for risk and liability management. This will involve:

- identification of risks – what are possible liabilities?
- evaluation of risks – what is probability of loss and severity of loss? and
- management of risks.

The strategy to be adopted will vary according to each charity's operations, but will include proper induction and training of trustees, good reporting procedures and financial controls, adequate systems for compliance and good records, indemnities, adequate and appropriate insurance. In addition, unincorporated charities should seek to limit contractual liability in contracts and may consider incorporation. Trustees must seek good professional legal and financial advice at the right time (i.e. not too late) from advisers with the necessary expertise.

Supervisory function

In addition to legal and financial responsibilities, trustees have a supervisory management function directed towards carrying out the charity's objectives. This includes responsibility for strategic planning, allocation of resources, quality management, policies, staff employment, board membership and succession, representation and advocacy.

Delegation of responsibility

Many of the issues to be considered relating to the proper financial management of the charity as a going concern have been discussed in *Chapter 3a* (from the viewpoint of the financial administrator). The strict legal rule is that trustees must act in person and decisions concerning the trustees must be taken by the trustees acting together.

The charity's governing document will often include a power for trustees to delegate their powers or duties to sub-committees. Where trustee decisions are delegated to sub-committees, these must always be on the terms that decisions are reported back fully and promptly to the full Board of Trustees. The powers and terms of reference of the sub-committee should be clearly defined and the delegation must be revocable by the trustees. A majority of members of the sub-committee should be trustees. Delegation should be confined to specific functions or duties, and excessive delegation which extended to a major part of the trustees' powers and duties could amount to a breach of trust.

In addition, trustees may delegate decisions on day-to-day management matters to employees. In practice, except in the smallest organisation, senior staff will do much of the work involved in discharging the trustees' responsibilities. Finance staff in particular will carry out much of the financial work. However, the principle is delegation *not abrogation*.

Trustees remain legally responsible, and must supervise and control the work of staff adequately. Decisions on certain financial issues including investment of surplus funds and disposal of significant assets must remain the collective responsibility of the trustees.

Position of the chair

There are two aspects of the role and duties of a chair. Firstly, the chair will normally plan and run the meetings of the trustees. Secondly, the chair will often have the important roles of liaising with the senior members of staff, particularly the chief executive, acting as a spokesperson for the trustees and charity, sometimes making essential or emergency decisions between trustee meetings, consulting with the other honorary officers and generally ensuring that the charity's policies and priorities are followed.

The treasurer's role

The treasurer (and for larger organisations, the chair of the finance sub-committee) will have specific responsibilities to act on behalf of the trustees to safeguard the organisation's finances. In a small charity, the treasurer will often deal with all aspects of finance and funding. In all charities, the treasurer will have the overview of financial planning and budgeting, financial reporting, funding and fundraising, banking, bookkeeping and record keeping. However, it is important to remember that *all* trustees remain legally responsible for the organisation's financial affairs. All trustees must be satisfied that they are receiving frequent (usually at least quarterly, and for larger organisations, monthly) financial information about the organisation.

In the case of charitable companies, the treasurer and chairman may sometimes be subject to a higher duty of care. The standard of care to avoid wrongful trading includes a subjective test so that the general knowledge, skill and experience that the individual director has will be taken into account. This will often mean that a duty of care higher than that required of the other trustees is imposed on the treasurer and chair for this purpose *(see Chapter 1)*.

Professional advisors

The trustees will often need to engage professional advisers to assist in discharge of their responsibilities. It is important to have as legal and financial advisers people with experience of charities. Purely commercial experience may not be sufficient. It is important that trustees should satisfy themselves that their advisers have the necessary experience and expertise in the area of charity law and practice. Expensive advice is not necessarily good advice. It is not a proper use of charity funds to spend large amounts on poor quality services.

Trustees cannot delegate decision making to advisers, and trustees cannot rely on professional advice to give complete protection from personal liability. However, if trustees take proper advice, this will be evidence that they have acted reasonably and prudently. And they may have an action for professional negligence, if the charity suffers financial loss as a result of bad advice.

It is particularly important for trustees to appoint as auditor someone who appreciates the issues and potential difficulties faced by the charity. Auditors should provide more than just an audit report to trustees, and should assist them in ensuring that their role of stewardship is discharged properly and effectively.

Holding trustees

Unincorporated organisations cannot own or hold property in their own name, and will have to appoint *holding trustees* to hold it on behalf of the organisation. Holding trustees are different from charity trustees. They have no management or financial responsibility for the charity or voluntary organisation as a whole.

Non-charities

Although trustees of charities have specific responsibilities under charity law and trust law, the same basic responsibilities apply to members of the management committee of a non-charitable voluntary organisation.

Where going concern status is questioned or the organisation is known to be insolvent

Where going concern status is questioned, there is a general duty for trustees to exercise particular vigilance and care. They must be aware of their duties regarding prudent financial management, the preservation of the organisation's assets and their responsibilities to meet commitments and to ensure continued operation of the organisation. They should seek appropriate legal and financial advice at an early stage. They should monitor the situation carefully and keep clear, detailed records of decisions and minutes of meetings. They should take all possible steps to raise funds, obtain alternative and/or additional sources of funding, reduce costs and cut back on expenditure, chase up debts, etc.

Where an organisation is known to be insolvent, trustees must take legal advice on their position and whether the organisation must be wound up. In the case of an unincorporated charity, the trustees may well be held personally liable for the debts of the organisation (*see personal liabilities below*). The trustees will need to take advice as to the correct procedures to follow. The procedures differ for incorporated and unincorporated organisations, and have been covered in *Chapter 2*.

In the case of a company limited by guarantee, trustees will be directors of the company and need to be aware of their position regarding wrongful trading – that is continuing to trade when knowing that the organisation is or is likely to become insolvent (*see Chapter 1*).

If there is real uncertainty as to solvency, it is important that the trustees should treat all the creditors fairly. In these circumstances the trustees should get help from a professional insolvency adviser to advise as to what continuing activities are in the interests of the creditors. It is critical to ensure that no payments are made to any creditors on an ad hoc basis and that there is no unfair preference of creditors.

Once a formal decision has been made to close down, the organisation exists only for the purpose of paying debts and dispersing its assets. Trustees must inform staff, advisers, creditors, beneficiaries (users), the Charity Commission, funders, etc. At this stage, every attempt must be made to preserve assets and cut overheads to a minimum.

Responsibilities towards staff and volunteers

Trustees have responsibilities to different groups which must be kept in balance. Although the overriding concern must be to carry out the objects of the charity and to preserve the charity assets, the trustees must also take into account responsibilities towards staff and volunteers. It is important that both the staff and volunteers should be involved in discussions and consultations where the organisation is facing financial difficulties.

Protective redundancy notices

Where there is a likelihood of loss of funding or deficiency in resources, trustees will need to consider issuing protective redundancy notices. These will cease to have effect should funding be forthcoming or if alternative sources of funding are found. The usual rules with regard to redundancy and procedures specified in the organisation's terms and conditions of employment, including the period of notice, will need to be followed. The trustees will need to observe consultation procedures laid down in the Employment Protection Act 1975 and the Employment Protection Consolidation Act 1978 and consult with the unions, the staff and in some cases the Department of Employment. The purpose of the protective redundancy notice is to protect the assets of the organisation and in some cases the personal liability of the trustees.

Staff morale

The question of issuing protective redundancy notices needs to be handled with sensitivity as it will obviously affect the morale of staff, and thus the efficiency and effectiveness of the organisation. Trustees should reassure staff by taking all possible steps to generate new resources to meet commitments and ensure continued operation of the organisation. They should also consider ways of avoiding redundancies such as short-time working, asking whether any staff wish to take early retirement or redeploying staff.

Statutory entitlements

Where attempts to secure alternative resources are unsuccessful and the organisation is closed down, redundancy issues need to be faced. Apart from the statutory entitlements to redundancy payments, contracts of employment will usually make provision for redundancy payments, which may give higher entitlements. These will be binding on trustees. Anything in addition to any contractual entitlement would be an ex gratia payment, and trustees should bear in mind the guidelines on making ex gratia payments issued by the Charity Commission before making any such payments (should the funds exist to do so).

Ex gratia payments

Redundancy payments and other payments to staff which are not non-contractual are subject to rules on ex gratia payments by charities. In some circumstances ex gratia non-contractual payments to staff can be treated as part of the charity's administration expenses. However, if the charity is to be wound up, such voluntary payments cannot be treated as ongoing administrative expenses for the charity, and clearance for making such payments will need to be obtained from the Charity Commission.

Volunteers

Although volunteers will not normally have the protection of employment legislation, they may well have terms and conditions for their volunteering which the trustees need to follow. Although trustees will not normally have legal obligations to volunteers, they should as far as possible take their interests into account and involve them in the consultation process. It is important for trustees to remember that volunteers have their own mental, emotional and sometimes even physical needs that are met by the charity.

Personal liabilities of the trustees

All trustees

Trustees can be personally liable in a number of different situations. The extent of liability will depend on the type of legal structure. All trustees are potentially personally liable for breach of trust regardless of legal structure. If for example they have failed in their duty to act as prudent businessmen and women with resulting loss to the charity, the Charity Commission or the court may call on them to make good the loss. Under Section 61 of the Trustee Act 1925, trustees can be relieved of liability for breach of trust if they have acted honestly and reasonably and ought fairly to be excused.

Trustees of unincorporated charities

In addition trustees of unincorporated charities can be held personally liable in contract or tort (a civil wrong such as negligence or nuisance). They will normally have a right of indemnity from the assets. (For incorporated charities, it is the organisation itself which is liable, not the trustees who are only liable up to the amount of the personal guarantee they have provided – usually a nominal £1.)

Where an unincorporated organisation becomes insolvent, the trustees (or members of the management committee) will be primarily liable for the organisation's debts. This liability exists regardless of whether they have acted reasonably, and Section 61 of the Trustee Act 1925 will afford them no protection. On an insolvency, potential areas of claims against trustees of unincorporated associations include liability under leases, under long-term contracts such as photocopier agreements and other hire agreements, and redundancy claims. The potential liability under these long-term agreements can be considerable.

In view of these potential liabilities, trustees of unincorporated charities need to take specific steps to protect their position, which can include:

- having clauses limiting liability included in leases and contracts

Case study 1:

The *holding trustees* of the charity constituted as an unincorporated association entered into a fifteen-year lease with a commercial landlord at an annual rental of £7,000. The lease contained no clause limiting the liability of the trustees. The association received the major part of its funding from the local authority on an annual basis. The funding was withdrawn as a result of the local authority's round of funding cuts, and the association closed down leaving a potential claim against the holding trustees as the lessees under the lease for a rental of £7,000 per annum for the balance of the term of the lease. The premises were in an inconvenient location and of limited general use, so it seemed unlikely that another lessee would be found to take over the lease. The case in fact had a happy ending, as after months of negotiation the landlord accepted a surrender. The case also raised interesting questions of how far the holding trustees, successfully sued by the landlord, could pursue either the members of the committee at the time the lease was signed or the current committee members for reimbursement of any sums paid.

- taking out adequate insurance
- having adequate reserves to cover contingencies.

In cases where an unincorporated organisation engages in substantial contracts and employs a number of staff, the trustees should consider incorporation. Where trustees are held personally liable for debts, the liability will be joint and several. This means all the trustees could be sued jointly or that one trustee could be sued for the whole amount of debt, but he or she would in turn be able to petition the Court for an equitable contributable from the other trustees if such a course of action was both practical and economical.

Trustees of incorporated charities

Case study 2:

A charity constituted as a trust had a board of trustees who were extremely busy people and, whilst being in sympathy with the objects, did not have the time to take an active part in the charity's affairs. They probably saw their role very much as patrons. In practice all decisions were made by the chief executive. The charity got into financial difficulties unbeknown to the trustees and many debts remained unpaid, but the chief executive hoped to raise more funds and rescue the situation. Finally, the trustees became aware of the true position, blew the whistle and the charity closed. The charity's creditors were able to pursue their claims (successfully) against the trustees, on the basis that the trustees should have made themselves aware of the charity's financial position.

Trustees of charities with limited liability (the most common structure being charitable companies limited by guarantee) will have initial protection against liability for the charity's debts by virtue of the incorporated status of the organisation.

Section 727 of the Companies Act 1985 provides that in proceedings for negligence, default, breach of duty or breach of trust against a director, the court may excuse a director if he or she has acted honestly and reasonably and ought fairly to be excused in whole or in part.

Trustees of charitable companies, as directors, will have potential personal liability for wrongful trading under the Insolvency Act 1986. If a claim for wrongful trading is upheld, the court may require the Directors to pay the sum to the company. They may also be disqualified from acting as company directors. Wrongful trading occurs if the company goes into insolvent liquidation, and at some time before the commencement of the winding up of the company, the director knew or ought to have concluded that there was no reasonable prospect that the company could avoid going into insolvent liquidation. A defence to such a claim is that the director took all steps to minimise loss to creditors. It appears that in this situation the obligation to run the company in the creditors' interests overrides any duties under charity law.

Continuing to trade whilst insolvent is not the same as wrongful trading. Provided that there is good evidence that a company which continues to trade will survive and pay its debts, the directors are unlikely to be held responsible. Good evidence would include credible financial forecasts demonstrating how the company will regain its solvency. The test of insolvency for the Act is that the company is unable to pay its debts. Inability to pay debts includes inability to pay debts as they fall due, and where the value of the assets is less than the liabilities, taking into account its contingent and prospective liabilities.

If the trustees are in a situation where a claim for wrongful trading could arise, they must take every step to monitor the charity's affairs very closely, they must hold frequent board meetings, and they must produce full detailed minutes of meetings to provide evidence that they have acted reasonably and properly in the conduct of company's affairs.

Personal liabilities of charity trustees – what can be done?

The personal liabilities that charity trustees are exposed to are extremely severe. The degree of risk depends on how the charity is constituted. The trustees of an incorporated charity are protected from any liability incurred by the charity through trading losses, claims and contractual obligations. The trustees of an unincorporated charity have no such protection, where all liabilities of the charity are assumed personally by the trustees. All trustees, however the charity is constituted, are exposed to personal liability arising from breach of trust, negligence and wrongful trading.

This exposure to personal liability can deter people from serving as trustees. And indeed if the extent of personal liability were widely known, it could frighten many serving trustees away. The best protection against liability is to ensure that the charity is run prudently and that it has or will have sufficient funds to meet all its obligations. There are a number of other ways in which trustees can seek to reduce their personal liability – through insurance, through contractual limitation and by incorporation.

Limiting liability by insurance

Some of the risks that charities face and which could force the charity into insolvency (if things were to go wrong) can be reduced by taking out appropriate insurance cover. This will also protect the trustees of unincorporated charities against personal liability. Whether or not it is worth taking out insurance will depend on the level of risk, the cost of the policy and the consequences for the charity if things were to go wrong. This is a matter of judgement for the trustees.

All charities (but especially unincorporated charities in view of the potential personal liability of the trustees) should consider the relevance of:

- **Public liability insurance;**
- **Product liability insurance** (if it is selling/manufacturing products);

- **Professional indemnity insurance** (if it is supplying services);
- **Defamation insurance** (if it is publishing material that could be libellous);
- **Fidelity insurance** (to protect the charity if an employee or trustee runs off with the charity's money);
- **Buildings and contents insurance** (to protect the charity from loss or damage to its property, bearing in mind that if it leases equipment the lease will almost certainly oblige the charity to insure the property);
- **Redundancy insurance** (to cover the cost of making employees redundant in the event of the organisation ceasing to trade).

Failure to insure might be held to constitute a breach of duty by the trustees, exposing them (however constituted) to personal liability. In the case of an unincorporated trust, failing to have adequate insurance could mean claims being made against the trustees personally, if the trust does not have sufficient assets to meet an uninsured claim.

One form of insurance policy – trustees indemnity insurance – covers certain risks to which charity trustees are exposed as a result of their trusteeship. This is a new area of cover that has recently become available. It is discussed in detail at the end of this chapter.

Limiting liability by contract

An effective way of limiting the personal liability of trustees of unincorporated charities is to seek to have written into any contract to which the charity is party that the liability of the charity trustees is limited to the assets of the charity, to the intent that the charity trustees shall incur no personal liability whatsoever.

When it is explained that charity trustees are volunteers who perform their task free, it is often possible to negotiate such a clause (e.g. for a lease of a building or a contract for the delivery of services). It is more difficult to do this when acquiring something on a standard form contract (e.g. the purchase of goods or the hire of a photocopier). It is straightforward to do when the charity is issuing its own contracts (e.g. in standard terms and conditions of employment for staff).

This mechanism for limiting the liability of trustees can only be used in the case of contracts. It does not limit the charity trustees' liability in relation to third parties not party to a contract – to cover some or all of these risks it is necessary to have proper insurance cover.

Limiting liability by incorporation

Incorporation creates a separate legal entity for the charity, and therefore contains any claims against the charity to what can be met out of the charity's own funds. Where a director of a charitable company agrees to give a personal guarantee for the obligations of the charity (for example under a lease or an overdraft), in such cases the director will be personally liable for any obligations entered into under the guarantee.

Because charity trustees of unincorporated charities have a greater exposure to risk if the charity becomes insolvent, as compared with the trustees of incorporated charities, it is worth considering whether to incorporate the charity to reduce the level of exposure to risk. An incorporated charity has slightly greater accounting and reporting obligations (under the Companies Acts and to Companies House) than unincorporated charities, which will involve more work and more cost. The process of conversion will involve some legal costs, as the original unincorporated charity will need to be wound up with its assets and obligations transferred to the new incorporated charity, and will also require the consent of the Charity Commissioners.

It will be worth considering incorporation where the trustees feel a need to limit their personal liability, and particularly where the affairs of the charity have become substantial and where the charity is incurring substantial obligations – contracts of employment, leases or buildings and equipment, agreements and contracts to provide services. If incorporation is considered, it also provides an opportunity for trustees to review their constitution and the powers available to them for running the charity and to bring these up to date with present requirements.

Trustees should note that incorporation does not remove all personal liability, and they might also wish to consider trustee liability insurance. Incorporation of the charity (as a company limited by guarantee or an industrial and provident society) should not be confused with incorporation of the trustees under the Charities Act 1993. Incorporation of the trustees does not limit the trustees' personal liability, it merely provides a simple mechanism for getting contracts and other documents signed.

Trustee liability insurance

A new area of insurance cover that has recently become available is trustee liability insurance. Trustee liability insurance policies offer cover to charity trustees (and this can be extended to employees such as the chief executive) against personal liability arising from breach of duty, breach of trust, negligence, error or omission or wrongful trading. The insurance cover will not protect the insured if they have been guilty of a criminal act or have acted deliberately or recklessly.

Such policies can be taken out by trustees with the insurance premiums paid for personally out of their own pockets without problem. Difficulties arise where the premiums are to be paid out of the charity's funds.

Trustee liability insurance became available partly as a result of Section 137 of the Companies Act 1989 which permitted insurance for company directors, officers and auditors, and the premiums to be paid out of company assets. The Charity Commission considered whether similar insurance could cover trustees, and in their Annual Review for 1991 stated that in appropriate cases they would permit a charity to pay for insurance for its trustees to cover personal liability for acts 'properly undertaken in the administration of a charity or undertaken in breach of trust but under an honest mistake'. It cannot be used to cover liability for actions that the trustees knew to be wrong.

However the Charity Commission went on to state that the insurance conferred a personal benefit to the trustees, so that special procedures need to be followed if the premiums are to be paid out of the charity's funds. In the case of an unincorporated charity wishing to take out trustee liability insurance, the trustees will need to obtain an Order from the Commissioners, unless there is an express power to provide trustee liability insurance in the charity's constitution. This is the case even if the charity has an amendments clause allowing the trustees to amend the constitution, as such a clause cannot be used to confer a benefit on the trustees. The trustees will need to show that the insurance is in the interest of the charity, and the Charity Commission will take into account the degree of risk, the nature of the charity's activities, the amount of indemnity required, the cost to the charity, and any special circumstances such as failure to find trustees because of exposure to personal liability.

In the case of a charitable company there will normally be a general power in the memorandum wide enough to cover taking out trustee liability insurance, but an amendment to the clause covering preclusion of personal benefit will normally be required. This amendment will require the prior written consent of the Commission. It appears that in all cases failure to obtain the consent of the Commission could result in a breach of trust.

The circumstances in which the Commission will permit charities to pay the costs of trustee liability insurance are currently under review. Before deciding to take out such a policy, trustees should check the current position with their legal adviser, or with the Trustee Services Unit of the National Council for Voluntary Organisations (071–713 6161), or with the Charity Commission itself.

Is it worth taking out trustee liability insurance? How do you decide? To answer the question you need to examine the liabilities the trustees face and assess the risk. It is important to look very closely at the cover afforded by the individual policy including any extensions and exclusions. It is worth looking at several different policies and deciding which is the right one for your charity, as the cover offered by the different policies varies considerably. In addition to cover indemnifying the trustees against personal liability, there will normally also be indemnity for losses occurring to the charity itself. The policy may also include professional indemnity or acts and omissions cover and indemnity for losses caused by the fraud of co-trustees. Alternatively professional indemnity cover may be included as an extension along with other areas such as legal expenses, loss of documents and unintentional breach of copyright.

CHAPTER 6

INSOLVENCY AND THE EFFECTIVE USE OF CHARITY FUNDS: A CHARITY COMMISSION PERSPECTIVE

BY R GREYHAM DAWES, FCA

The Charity Commissioners' aim of promoting the efficient use of charitable funds does not concern only the protection of charity assets and their proper application in accordance with the terms of trust. It concerns the entire administration of the charity – including the management of any liabilities incurred by the trustees.

Although the Commission must not itself become involved in charity administration, it can and does investigate and intervene to stop abuse, inefficiency or neglect by charity trustees. Some of the Commission's particular concerns are discussed below.

Borrowings

Charity activities are normally expected to be funded wholly out of income of the current year, with any deficit being made good out of income surpluses from previous years. Capital expenditure and other special projects, however, often cannot be funded in this way. Unless they can raise the extra money from duly authorised internal borrowing from an endowment or from the proceeds of fundraising appeals, the trustees may conclude that they must borrow externally. In many cases this can take the form of 'soft loans' from supporters of the charity – typically interest-free and repayable by mutual agreement. Where such advantageous terms are not possible, commercial loans may be the only alternative.

Because of the inherent risks involved in taking on commercial debt of any kind, the Charity Commission will always want to see any such external borrowing kept to a minimum, with the borrowing terms as much as possible to the charity's advantage. This is seen as particularly important for loans from 'connected persons' (i.e. close family and business connections of the trustees).

Future income prospects and the charity's ability to repay the capital as well as the interest on the loan need to be regularly reassessed. This is even more essential where the borrowing is used to cover operational deficits rather than to fund capital expenditure. In a recent case, an educational charity had fallen into the habit of relying on larger and larger bank overdrafts secured on the school premises to keep its school going from term to term during the recession. At the point where the borrowing had to be consolidated into a fixed-term loan, the school suffered a sharp fall in expected new pupils due to cuts in the armed forces and was therefore unable to demonstrate a viable repayment plan. The only remaining option in such a case may be to shut down part of the charity's activities and sell assets in order to reduce the debt. Even this may not work unless it is done in good time and without undue haste.

Coping with a downturn

In trying to cope with the effects of severe recession, trustees may have borrowed heavily to maintain the level or scale of service previously provided by the charity. Or in having to curtail activities in order to reduce their costs, they may have exposed themselves to substantial claims by employees, suppliers, etc. In both cases the Commission's concern is that the trustees should achieve a reasonable balance between the needs of present and the future beneficiaries of the charity, and the wishes and justifiable expectations of its existing donors. As a trustee you should therefore always obtain competent advice where you face difficulties and difficult decisions, and are not sure what to do for the best. This must be done in good time if you are to have any prospect of retrieving the situation without loss to yourself.

Insolvency

While the Commission does have an interest in helping charity trustees avoid the personal difficulties which can arise in insolvency situations, so that they should not be discouraged from acting as trustees, its primary concern is with the taking of measures:

- to restore the financial viability of the charity so that its activities can continue, or (if that is not feasible)
- to reduce the risk to charity assets from the continuation of activities which are not sustainable in the longer term,
- (in a salvage situation) to prevent charity assets being used by creditors or trustees to redeem losses or settle liabilities which are properly theirs personally, and
- to provide for alternative ways for those assets to be ultimately applied for appropriate charitable purposes.

The Commission will also be concerned to quantify any liabilities for breach of trust and to pursue them, if there is a real prospect of funds ultimately being made available for further charitable purposes, rather than merely for the benefit of charity creditors.

Insolvency may or may not be the result of maladministration. It does not necessarily put charity property at risk, and so invoke the Commission's supervisory role. It may simply be the result of unexpected withdrawal of funding support for charitable services which the trustees have committed themselves to provide. In adjusting to the new situation, the trustees may need to consult the Commission's Charity Support Division in order to obtain confirmation that any structural and constitutional changes they propose to make are considered reasonable and proper in the circumstances; or, in certain cases, to obtain formal consent to such changes.

If the charity runs out of funds completely and ceases to operate or even to exist, it will then be removed from the charities register.

Avoiding personal liability for trustees

Charity insolvency primarily threatens loss to its creditors and, in certain cases, to the trustees. The trustees of an unincorporated charity remain personally liable in law on all contracts into which they have entered on its behalf, except where the terms of the contract expressly limit this personal liability to the value of the charity's assets. They sometimes do not fully appreciate that their personal assets are exposed to the claims of creditors, if the charity's assets are insufficient.

A trustee acting properly will usually have a claim over the charity's assets to indemnify himself or herself against any liabilities to which he or she is subject as a trustee, but it is no concern of the creditor if these assets are insufficient to satisfy the trustee's claim. In practice, this means that charity solvency here is an internal matter between the trustees themselves, and does not directly concern the creditor.

In the case of the forced closure of a charity school in Avon, for instance, the trustees were obliged to make good out of their own pockets the net deficiency remaining when the sale of all the charity's assets was insufficient to meet all its liabilities.

The trustees of an unincorporated charity should thus always ensure that for each trust administered by them current assets exceed short-term liabilities in terms of expected cash availability, and also that total assets exceed total liabilities in terms of net realisable values, if they wish to avoid the possibility that the charity's creditors may gain access to their personal assets, whether via bankruptcy proceedings or otherwise.

Liquidity and solvency

In examining a charity's accounts to ascertain its financial position, the Charity Commission is also concerned to see that 'liquid assets' (cash, short-term debtors and easily marketable investments or other non-fixed assets) appear to be of sufficient value to cover all short term liabilities, and whether total assets appear sufficient to meet total liabilities (including the obligation to discharge any special trusts) in the long term – i.e. beyond the following financial year.

The position is not so simple where a charity includes substantial 'special trusts'. As their unexpended assets must not be used for purposes other than those stipulated, the liquidity and long-term solvency positions must be calculated separately for each fund. Any apparent deficits are liable to investigation as possible breaches of trust.

The financial position of the charity

Because the ultimate financial strength or weakness of the charity sometimes cannot be assessed simply from the balance sheet and explanatory notes, the Commission may from time to time ask the trustees to provide supplementary information concerned such matters as (for example):

- Any substantial difference between the book value of certain major assets and their realisable market value;
- Any major potential and contingent liabilities – some of which would crystallise only on a winding up (staff redundancy, contract termination claims, grant repayment claims, etc.) -not adequately disclosed in the accounts;
- Any reserve funding commitments made by supporters of an apparently insolvent charity to trustees who may be depending on last-minute appeals to such donors to rescue it in times of financial crisis;
- In the case of accounts qualified by the auditor or examiner disagreeing with the 'going concern' basis of their preparation, to what extent the trustees are able to justify maintaining the charity's activity levels in the face of impending or potential insolvency;
- To what extent the assets and liabilities of special trusts not sufficiently analysed in the accounts have been segregated in the administration of the charity in order to avoid their being used to fund a deficit elsewhere among the charity's funds.

Where the audited accounts indicate that a charity of sufficient for the Commission to be concerned may be or become insolvent, the Commission will require explanations and assurances from the trustees and may then initiate remedial action. As a trustee in such a situation you should always be aware of the need to seek professional advice of your own, and if in doubt about your own solvency you should also consult an insolvency practitioner.

For an incorporated charity, where it is decided that the organisation must be wound up and the directors cannot provide the required statutory declaration of the company's solvency, or the liquidator discovers that the company is insolvent, the creditors take charge of the winding up process, or the court may be petitioned under Section 122 to wind up the company. Alternatively under Section 63, Charities Act 1993, the

Commissioners may, with the agreement of the Attorney General, petition for the winding up of the company.

The Charity Commission carries out much the same kind of check on the balance sheet and auditor's report of a charitable company as for an unincorporated charity. In the absence of fraudulent or wrongful trading, the directors will not generally be liable for the charity's debts unless they have personally guaranteed them. They may therefore not feel under quite the same compulsion to see to its rescue in times of financial crisis. On the other hand, the 'foresight test' under Section 214 of the Insolvency Act for the ascertainment of the extent of a director's personal liability is particularly important in the case of major companies providing charitable services dependent on grants or subsidies, and is felt to be onerous enough to compel the directors in most cases to take proper care over their charity's financial situation.

Monitoring and supervision by the Commission

The monitoring of charity performance by the Charity Commission, including (as one element) the analysis of annual accounts received for filing, is a relatively recent development arising from computerisation of the Charities Register. The monitoring function provides information to enable the Commission to maintain a pro-active stance in the regulation of charities.

Annual Returns are being used to gather selected information from the trustees for a database associated with the computerised register. Unlike the Basic Register Index (the charities register) the data held in the Monitoring Database is not available to the public. By comparing charities with features in common, those which do not conform to normal expectations can be singled out for closer inspection – initially of their accounts. Supplementary questionnaires may then be used to determine, on the basis of the trustees' response, whether the case is one which should be handled by the Charity Support Division or the Charity Supervision Division. In this way, the Commission's resources can be concentrated more and more on helping charities in need, rather than those which are adequately self-regulated.

Trustees may apply in writing to the Commissioners for their opinion or advice under Section 29, Charities Act 1993 on any matter affecting the performance of their duties. Provided they have taken care to ensure that all material facts of the case were disclosed and the matter was not the subject of court action, the trustees can safely act on the opinion or advice thus received. This is a valuable safeguard for trustees in any situation, including insolvency.

The Commissioners have extensive powers of intervention under Sections 18 and 19 of the Charities Act to protect charity property or to deal with maladministration where it is deemed necessary to use such powers. These include suspending and removing trustees, officers, agents and employees of the charity, restricting dealings in charity property and enforcing its transfer to the Official Custodian, appointing receivers and managers and additional trustees, and establishing charity administration schemes.

PART 2

PRACTICAL METHODS FOR DEALING WITH FINANCIAL WEAKNESS

CHAPTER 7

MANAGEMENT AND FUNDRAISING TO AVOID CRISIS

BY MICHAEL NORTON

The most obvious strategy for a financial crisis is to ensure that you never get to a point of crisis in the first place! This chapter has some thoughts on how to prevent a crisis, and on what to do if you do find yourself in a crisis situation.

Early diagnosis

The sooner you are alerted to a deteriorating position, the better it will be and the more time you will have to rectify the situation. So it is sensible to look out for indicators of problems over the horizon. The sorts of things you might look out for include:

- One or more long-standing funding bodies or supporters not renewing their grants, when they were expected to do so;
- Attendance at management committee meetings beginning to fall away. People lose interest or are disheartened at what they feel in the current state of affairs;
- Good committee members, who have in the past done a great deal for the organisation, finding that they no longer have the time to commit;
- Increased absenteeism and staff sickness – through stress, lack of leadership and proper management, or loss of commitment to the organisation;
- Good staff looking for and perhaps finding other jobs;
- The cash position becoming increasingly tight – and even the non-financial amongst the trustees begin to be aware that something is going wrong.

Taken individually none of these may be significant. Nor might some of the other changes you begin to spot. There may be perfectly good reasons for what is happening. But a number of small changes happening at about the same time can add up to a warning of an impending crisis.

The key is to spot the pattern and realise that something is up. If a crisis is looming it is also important to be able to identify the underlying problem, the primary cause of what is taking place. It is only then that it is possible to develop an action plan to deal with the problem.

Better management control

One common cause of a crisis is inadequate management and financial information, so that you are unable to keep track of the organisation's financial position and to know that you are edging towards or have already reached a crisis. It is important, therefore, to have proper up-to-date information.

The organisation, its trustees or members of the management committee and its senior staff, should all assure themselves that the organisation is operating properly. This includes the following steps.

- The systems used for producing financial information and monitoring performance should be adequate. This includes monitoring the performance of branches and trading subsidiaries where the performance of these will materially affect the overall position of the organisation. If there is any doubt about the organisation's financial position, professional advice should be taken immediately. If there are any material changes in the way in which the organisation operates or in how it is financed, new systems may be needed or current practice may need to be reviewed. In any case, it is wise to ask the auditors for a management letter each year, which will give their comments on how well the existing financial systems are working, and what could be done to improve them.

- Any qualitative information *(see Chapter 4)* that is being produced should support the view of the organisation provided by the quantitative (accounting) information.

- The process of reviewing the financial position should be well understood by those who are doing it, and the procedures for doing so should allow for regular scrutiny of information produced on time, with a report outlining the current position and putting forward recommendations for action, where appropriate. If anyone has any doubts about the financial status of the organisation, they should be encouraged to speak out, not keep quiet.

- Major items that will affect the charity's financial position, including major payments that are due, risks of loss of income, other liabilities, potential liabilities and contingent liabilities should be known about in good time. These items should be listed, and if they are likely to create problems, a close watch should be kept on the situation. The monthly accounts may show 'calm waters', but there may be 'icebergs' ahead!

- Proper note should be taken when reviewing the financial position of any restricted funds which have been raised and must be spent for a particular purpose. The income position and the cash position of the organisation may appear healthy, but this may mask a situation where the income and cash available to meet the general expenditure of the organisation may be seriously in deficit.

- The trustees should give sufficient time to discussing the *longer-term strategy* of the organisation and its *funding implications*, as well as on the management and review of *current performance*. This might include strategy planning days, three or even five-year rolling budgets, external reviews of the charity's long-term potential. Keeping an eye on the future enables you to deal with potential problems while there is still time to do this, and to develop long-term sources of income to meet your future expenditure plans.

There should be sufficient financial competence amongst the trustees and committees members, the chief executive and the financial staff to be able to understand and interpret the management information that is being produced. Where this is not the case, the situation should be remedied.

Eight common problems

There are all sorts of reasons why organisations get into trouble. Here are a few. It is worth trying to identify which (if any) are relevant to you, and what you might do to prevent them occurring.

1. Loss of vision

Most organisations when they start out have a central vision, a sense of purpose and the enthusiasm and commitment of a small group of people, who know exactly what they want to do and are prepared to give up their time and energies to do it or to see it done. Over the years, this commitment may vanish, and the organisation may lose its way. Trustees, employed staff and volunteers may all feel a sense of malaise or purposelessness. It may even be worse than this, with everyone's energies consumed on bickering and squabbling amongst themselves. It is precisely at this time that a renewal is needed, with a sense of common purpose injected into the organisation and a recognition that the role of the organisation is as relevant today as when it was first set up. There are many different ways of doing this. But recognising the problem and that something must be done about it is the first step.

2. Loss of core funding

One of the most common reasons for financial failure is the loss of a major grant, which has underpinned the work of the organisation and without which the organisation is no longer viable (at least in its present form). Typically, it is a local authority or another statutory funding body which is trying to reduce its funding commitment. Often this is as a result of external factors, such as a squeeze on their own grants budgets. There are a number of steps that can be taken *before* such a situation arises:

- Build good working relationships with your funders, with regular contact and feedback to show that you are meeting the need effectively and efficiently. Get them to understand that the needs are important, long-term and of common concern, and that it is in everybody's interests that the service be able to continue;

- Try to obtain longer-term funding arrangements (such as a three-year grant commitment) and to insist that any notification of a cut (if costs have to be made) is given in sufficient time for you to be able to do something about it;
- Diversify your funding sources, so that you are not over-reliant on any one grant;
- Develop a contingency plan for dealing with this particular loss of grant.

3. Loss of project funding

Many organisations fund themselves by undertaking projects and allocating a slice of the central administrative expenditure of the organisation to each of the projects. This strategy may meet their immediate funding needs, but can pose a strain on the fundraising, which needs continually to come up with money to fund the projects. If a project ends and is not replaced with another, or if a funding programme which has been providing support terminates, this can reduce the overall work of the organisation and mean that the allocations towards central administrative expenditure are no longer sufficient to meet the central costs.

It may be that the central costs can be reduced (in line with the reduced work programme). It may be, however, that they are largely fixed (the cost of the director, the financial administration, the convening of trustees' meetings, office costs will all remain the same). In such circumstances, the loss of one grant can trigger a 'domino effect' creating financial problems for the organisation as a whole. There are a number of ways of coping with this:

- Allocate more than 100% of the budgeted central costs on to the projects you are running. This means a larger allocation per project. You can then spend some of the additional central costs on research, development, marketing or other costs which could be cut back if and when resources come under pressure. This will inject some 'fat' into the system. But it will also enhance your work through spending more on its development.
- Have a number of new projects ready and waiting with their funding more or less in place, which could be brought on stream earlier if the need arises.
- Attract more funding and new sources of support for your current projects to allow them to continue beyond their current funding phase.

4. Short-term funding for long-term needs

Many organisations have continuing commitments – to their beneficiaries, to keep a building in operation, to see a work programme through. But at the same time, they have adopted an essentially short-term approach to their fundraising, raising the money they need year by year, and spending everything they raise each year. This means that at the beginning of each year, the fundraising has to begin largely from scratch.

If funds become harder to raise or if traditional funding sources dry up, this short-term approach to fundraising can create problems. If the money can't be raised or can't be raised in time, the work programme has to be cut, or a deficit run up, which can be the beginning of a crisis.

If you are there for the long term, it is important to develop long-term sources of income, which can inject stability and confidence into the planning and development of the organisation's work. Some ideas are given at the end of this chapter of ways of developing a longer-term approach to your fundraising.

5. No reserves

Many organisations have a considerable expenditure each year, but little in the way of assets or reserves. This means that if things go wrong there is little or no leeway. One view often taken is that if money is desperately needed, then it can be raised... then when it is actually needed. But it might be that if the situation is desperate for whatever reason (the roof has fallen in, a major supporter has gone broke, the Council has cut its grant budget completely), it will be much harder to raise money to a deadline than when you have the luxury of time on your side. The question of developing reserves as a buffer against financial crisis is discussed in *Chapter 5*.

6. Undercosting your applications

A very common cause of financial problems is that the fundraising budgets have been undercosted. This might simply be because an item (such as insurance or training) has been left out. But more often it is the result of a process which goes something like this:

'Funding is hard, and the funder is getting far more applications than can be supported... If we produce a lower budget for the project, we stand a better chance of getting support... and our project will appear to be that much more cost effective.'

But this is a recipe for disaster. Costs are costs. When the expenditure is incurred, it has to be paid for. If the money isn't there, it will create a (larger) deficit. It is far better to cost your projects accurately, including all costs, allowing for marketing, development and dissemination (which will all cost money), covering the costs of depreciation and use of equipment, contributing sufficiently towards the central costs, and even leaving something towards contingencies. Although this will create a larger budget for the project, it is better to do this and to concentrate on the value of the project and its cost-effectiveness – to 'sell it' on its worth not on its cheapness.

7. A Marketing Problem

Today's voluntary organisation is often funded from a variety of sources and may be 'earning' a good part of its budget through selling its services (bed spaces at a hostel, training places, gate receipts etc.). You may find that you are not meeting your financial targets because people are not purchasing your services. This creates a double problem: a loss of income and a sense that the service is no longer needed or working properly. If this happens, you have a marketing problem rather than a fundraising problem.

You could try to fundraise to meet the deficit. But you might try to take a more entrepreneurial approach, finding new ways of promoting your service, developing closer and more contractual relationships with your major customers, or filling empty places through 'special offers'.

8. Failure to adapt

The environment in which we all work is changing very rapidly. New needs are emerging all the time. New ways of working are being developed. Statutory funding programmes change. Funders respond to new fashions and develop new priorities for their grant-making. New funding partnerships are being created between 'purchasers' and 'providers' for the delivery of service. The block grant is being replaced by a service agreement or by multiple funding from a variety of different sources all with an interest in the problem. This process of change will continue, and may even accelerate.

An organisation stuck in the past, which fails to adapt to these changes, may find itself overtaken by events. There may be other, livelier, newer, more adaptable organisations that have seen change as an opportunity, that have met the challenge of change and have become more effective than you. They are attracting the funders, the supporters, the volunteers, the publicity... and not you.

This gets back to *Point 1*. You may not have lost your sense of vision. But your vision has increasingly become out of date. A process of renewal is needed. A new strategy, not just for surviving but for being successful, needs to be developed.

Developing an action plan

One of the best ways to get to the bottom of the problem is to identify a small group of talented people (possibly from both staff and trustees) to discuss the issues and develop a diagnosis. This group is then well placed to develop an action plan to address the problem.

This group could either be very informal, meeting around the director's kitchen table on Saturday mornings, or more formal, approved by the trustees as an 'action group'. It may well be that the action group needs to meet on a weekly basis to develop the plan and to start implementation of agreed actions. Time is critical in a crisis situation. The faster the group can work, the more they will gain control over their circumstances.

Good communication

During this time, substantially increased effort will be required to keep everyone in the organisation informed of actions and progress. It may be that the director will need to meet staff weekly to update them on developments. It may be that the director should write to trustees every other week to keep them informed of progress. All of this will help to give people confidence that the crisis is being contained, and that their futures will be secured.

One particularly difficult aspect of a crisis is redundancy. If this is necessary, it is usually best to get it all out of the way in one go, and not to have a number of announcements on separate occasions which make everyone feel insecure.

Role of the director

In an organisation with employed staff, the director or senior staff member is central to the turnaround. This person needs to lead the organisation out of the crisis. He or she will require a clear remit from trustees, and clear boundaries within which action can be taken should be set. The director will need to demonstrate to staff that the problem has been diagnosed and that he or she, with the trustees, is actively implementing a 'rescue' plan. This may entail the director/co-ordinator being more decisive and not being in a position of having to consult with everyone on all decisions.

Role of the chair

The chair also has a key role to play in overcoming a crisis. The first role is to support the director and work closely with him/her throughout the difficult period. The chair should also take responsibility for putting extra effort into keeping trustees informed of the problem and the actions that are being taken. Good communications are an essential ingredient of keeping the confidence of trustees during difficult periods.

Eight possible solutions

If you do find yourselves moving towards a position of financial crisis, you may need to do something quickly. Early action is important, as the situation is only likely to get worse. And if you do get into a position of actual crisis, it may then be too late to retrieve the situation. There may not be time to think or act strategically, and people may have become locked into fixed positions (often blaming everyone else for the crisis). Here are a few suggestions for some things you might do.

1. Audit your achievements

Look at the need, why it is important and why it is urgent to do something about it. Look at the achievements of the organisation, what you have done, how much you have done, what you have achieved, particular successes, case study examples that demonstrate your effectiveness, what would have happened if you had not been there. This can all rekindle a sense of worth in yourselves and in your organisation, which is particularly important at a time when you might all be feeling demoralised.

Look at your future plans, at how innovative or special your work is, at projects or developments which are of particular relevance now, at the importance of your being able to continue. Fire yourselves with enthusiasm for your 'mission' and the value of the work you hope to do. This enthusiasm will help you negotiate yourselves out of the problem.

2. Consult your stakeholders

Your major funders, your volunteers, your members and donors are all partners with you. They have *chosen* to give their money and their time to your work. They have demonstrated their commitment to the importance of the problem and the need to do something. They have stated their confidence that you are the organisation to do something about it.

This existing commitment should be seen as an asset, something in reserve to draw on if things are going wrong.

Develop a strategy for survival. Involve them in the discussions, ask them to make an investment in your future (which will add value to the investment they have already made in you). Bring your key supporters together to a 'round table' to discuss the problems and the solutions. You may feel that you are no longer very fundable, but they may feel that it is crucial that you pull through. And they may be able to help or to help you find ways of doing this.

3. Cut costs, enhance income, improve cash flow

This is the traditional approach to a financial crisis. Cutting your costs, especially cutting out waste; enhancing your income, by doubling your fundraising efforts or by marketing your services more effectively; improving your cash flow, particularly by collecting any money due to you as early as possible: these will all stop the drain on your resources and bring in more money now.

This may be easier said than done. But immediately you have decided that there is a financial problem or a crisis, you need to think about what action you can take in each of these three categories. You may develop some quite radical ideas – new approaches to dealing with the problem, completely new ways of working, making more use of volunteers – as well as the more usual ideas of saving on the phone bill or sending out invoice reminders earlier.

4. Appeal to existing supporters for more support

Crisis fundraising is hard, because successful fundraising relationships take time to develop. It is hard to raise large amounts of money unless you do the groundwork first. But you can appeal to your existing members and supporters for help to tide you over. This could be through an additional donation, or it could be by lending you money (interest free) for the time being. It may be, too, that if you can first persuade a few key supporters to back you that this will help persuade others to follow suit.

5. Expand your way out of failure

An impending crisis may jolt you into the view not just that you must do better, but that you must do more. It may provide you with an opportunity to expand your horizons – to develop and bring on stream new projects now, which will contribute more towards the administrative costs, or to go for a large capital appeal to improve your facilities or create a capital fund. Now may be the time to expand, not contract. And the process of expansion will restore you to financial viability and health. However, before considering this option, it is important to ensure that the organisation is financially viable. Taking on the risks of expansion, if the consequences are not properly thought through, could be seen as financially irresponsible.

6. Investment options

Investment is a process well understood in business, but little used in charities. The process is simple: spend money now, to generate income or save costs later. It has a particular twist for charities, in that they can 'package' up the investment costs into a fundraising application, so that the immediate costs are underwritten, and the benefits that will accrue in time will transform the charity's future financial position.

There are many ideas for investment. Here are a few, but you will have to find examples which are relevant to you, now. Investing in your premises so that you can rent them out for meetings or use them for training. Investing in a legacy campaign (the people you will ask for a legacy do not conveniently die just afterwards). Investing in technology to improve your effectiveness. Investing in marketing and PR to make you more fundable. Investing in that brilliant fundraising idea or work project which will prove a sure fire winner.

Each project (and there could be more than one) must be properly costed (and not undercosted) with an appropriate allocation towards central costs. The value of the investment can be assessed not only in relation to the worth of the work you are doing, but in the multiplier effect of the resources it will bring in later. This approach to fundraising and development will improve your immediate income. It will also enhance your future prospects.

7. Collaboration and partnership

There is a constant complaint from funders that there are 'too many charities all doing the same thing'. This may not often be true. But it is certainly that there are many opportunities for collaboration and partnership – between charities, and also between charities and statutory providers. Such collaboration can bring the complementary strengths of two organisations to bear on the project or problem. It can share costs and administration. It can develop a better service. It can demonstrate to funders the value of the collaboration and the benefit of the individual contributions. Collaboration can create better services, save money and make your project more fundable.

8. New blood at the head of the organisation

A financial crisis provides a good opportunity to review the contribution of those charged with the supervision and stewardship of the organisation – the trustees, the board members or the management committee. These are the people who have been selected or elected, or who have put themselves forward to lead the organisation.

The crisis may throw up the fact that they are not succeeding, that they do not possess all the skills or the contacts needed to be successful, and that you need new blood at the helm – to add to or to replace those already there. A change at the top can help create a renewed sense of enthusiasm, develop new and radical ideas for the future of the organisation, and be just the medicine that the organisation needs to restore it to financial health.

It is also possible that senior staff have become 'burned out', or that they have not adapted to the new environment within which voluntary organisations operate. They may be holding back the organisation, or may be putting the management committee members at risk by not providing adequate information about the organisation, its finances and its prospects. In this situation it may be necessary for the trustees or management committee to take steps to ensure they get the information they need and/or to provide support or training to help senior staff to manage better.

THREE CASE STUDIES

A metropolitan Citizens Advice Bureau

This CAB derived over 95% of its income from one large grant from the local Council. But over the past three years, the grant had been reduced – in actual terms, but even more so in real terms. Since 85% of total costs were absorbed by salaries and associated costs (an application of largely human resources to human problems), there was little scope for cutting costs other than by cutting services. The management group had a policy of 'no volunteers', holding that only professionally qualified and paid staff could deliver the quality of service needed. Their attempts to extend funding had been half-hearted, and the main thrust of their fundraising effect was on lobbying the local council. If current trends were to continue, the organisation would have to reduce opening hours, close branches, curtail its services at a time when more and more people are in need of them. The funder supports the work of the organisation with a half million pound grant. But it is itself under considerable pressure to reduce its own grants budget.

Comment: In this actual case, the management group did agree (but not unanimously, or with any real enthusiasm) that something needed to be done. A range of new fundraising opportunities and partnerships were drawn up. But the organisation had no experience and little competence in implementing this, and the action taken had only a marginal success on improving the position. There was no change in the policy on volunteers. The result has been that the process of decline and curtailment of services has continued. Perhaps it is easier for an outsider to see the extent of the problems, to generate solutions and to find ways of putting these ideas into practice. But it is up to the trustees or management group itself to take the initiative at as early a stage as possible in developing a turnaround strategy and in seeing it implemented.

Scottish Enterprise Trusts

Enterprise trusts were established during the 1980s as a partnership between business and local government to promote and support new business and to provide skills training. By the early 1990s, the increase in unemployment had made the problem that the enterprise trusts were trying to address more acute. The problem was that funding was getting harder and harder. Companies and local authorities were no longer seeking it as a 'partnership' to solve a problem, but as just another request for funds. Some trusts still retained strong support from these traditional sources. Some had developed alternative sources – particularly from managing training programmes, from the European Social Fund or through income generation schemes such as running business fairs or managed workspace. A few of the trusts were in financial trouble.

Comment: With over 30 enterprise trusts in Scotland, there were some remarkable examples of successful programmes and fundraising schemes. One strategy for those finding the going difficult might be to share the examples and ideas of more successful Trusts. A second would be to renew the sense of partnership by bringing the stakeholders together (business and local authorities) and asking them to confirm their commitment to the cause and to working together on the solution. A third would be to explore ideas for support in kind (from both sides of the partnership) at a time when cash donating budgets were under strain. A fourth would be to explore new strategies for dealing with the problems of unemployment which had increased threefold since the enterprise trust movement had started, to develop new ideas and new solutions for the 1990s, and to use these as the basis of a fundraising drive.

The Theatre Girls Club

A long-established hostel for homeless women in Soho, this organisation was getting into financial difficulties towards the end of the 1970s. Its lease was also running out. It could have gone into liquidation, owing some £30,000 to the Inland Revenue and other creditors. But there was a recognition of the need for the service, the special needs that the hostel was meeting, the competence of the staff. A round table discussion amongst stakeholders led to a rescue plan. A local housing association was able to purchase the hostel building and obtain funding from the Housing Corporation for its development and future management. The Greater London Council provided alternative premises to keep a skeleton service going during the redevelopment. A prominent trust paid off the accumulated debt on the strength of the rescue plan, with the proviso that an experienced financial consultant be drafted in as adviser. The main 'top up' funders committed themselves to continuing funding for the project.

Comment: A successful example of a technically bankrupt organisation expanding itself out of failure, rather than go into liquidation.

Fundraising solutions

There are two approaches to developing a strong and successful organisation. One is through good management and good planning; the other is through the development of successful fundraising. This section looks briefly at some of the fundraising issues and ideas.

Costing projects and contracts adequately

As has been mentioned before, a prime cause of financial weakness is the undercosting of projects. All projects should be carefully costed to include:

- The (actual) direct costs of running the project;
- A reasonable allocation towards the central administrative costs of running the organisation;
- The real cost of using assets (depreciation, asset replacement provisions, wear and tear);
- Any hidden subsidies, such as rent-free premises, should be identified and noted;
- Sundry costs for items that will inevitably be incurred, but which are often forgotten, such as computer training and new software;
- The cost of research and development, dissemination and promotion, publicity and PR, which help develop the organisation and build its future;
- The cost of raising the money (which will probably be included as a central cost);
- A surplus toward contingencies and to help build reserves (which will not necessarily appear as such).

Every cost has to be justifiable and justified. But the cost of every item that is incurred must come from somewhere. It will be the work of a successful fundraiser to create fundraising budgets which meet the financial needs of the projects and of the organisation itself, which will then be used to set the fundraising targets. The successful fundraiser will then make sure that these targets are met.

Developing a successful fundraising approach

With a good cause, a successful organisation and a track record of high quality work, fundraising should be easy – if the essential resources are brought together. Too often, organisations simply fire off their applications to the latest list of grant sources they can get their hands on, rather than thinking the process through. To enhance your chances of success, you will need:

- A fundraising **strategy** appropriate to your organisation. Whether you are supported from statutory grants, by a group of active members and donors, through successful fundraising events, from legacies or sponsorship, or from the income you earn, you need to have thought through how you want your organisation to be funded.

- The right **resources**: which includes technical skills, information, contacts and good personal and working relationships, equipment, systems for asking, receiving and thanking, literature and handouts, people to do the work with energy, enthusiasm for the job and commitment to the cause.

- Sufficient **time**: it always takes longer to raise money successfully, and the longer you give yourself the more successful you are likely to be.

- And **money**: A professional approach to fundraising will look at the inputs (how much money and time has to be invested), the timescale (how long it will take to get a return), the return (in terms of immediate support and the stream of income that might develop over the years). It is obviously important to keep fundraising costs low, but it is also evident that money may need to be invested now in the expectation of generating a successful return later. The trustees need to understand this investment process and to provide sufficient resources to the person they have entrusted to do a good job.

Developing long-term relationships

The essence of successful fundraising is to develop a core of committed support from people and institutions who share your concern for the cause and who believe in your abilities to do something about it. These people need to be identified and then nurtured. They are not just donors, but partners. You need to look at ways of cementing a relationship with them through reporting back and personal contact. The cost of fundraising from people who have already demonstrated their support for you is an order of magnitude lower than finding new supporters. Yet most fundraisers spend most of their time looking for new supporters and new sources of support. Of course you must spend some time doing this, but you must also:

• Invest time and effort in sustaining your existing donor and supporter list;

• Develop fundraising initiatives which can be repeated, and which, through good management and by learning from experience, become more and more successful each year;

• Devise structures for encouraging regular committed giving – service agreements with your main funders, covenant and membership schemes for individual donors, long-term partnerships with key supporters;

• Never believe that someone wants to give just once. People want to support you because they believe in your work, because you need the money and because you ask and have put forward a good case for support. If you need more money or money for other things, if you ask effectively, they may want to support you again.

Income generation

Many of today's organisations raise some or much of their money by selling their services – either direct to the beneficiaries or to purchasing bodies (such as local and health authorities). Fundraising is no longer asking for money, but selling a service on the quality of the service and its cost. This is marketing rather than fundraising. New skills are needed if what you are running is in essence a business activity. And new financial structures are needed to cope with investment, development, marketing and risk – all alien concepts in a grants culture. If you are operating within this new culture, you must ensure that you have or acquire the skills and expertise to be successful.

The value of volunteers

One added resource that many charities bring to their work is the time and commitment of volunteers. The value of the volunteer traditionally has not appeared in charity accounts, and so has been undervalued. Overall, volunteers commit as much to charity through the time they give as the public does through the donations they make. Yet voluntary work and the volunteer input is often seen as the poor relation to fundraising. It is a sensible strategy to define an effective role for volunteers with your organisation, and then:

• Value the volunteer input in cash terms (at £3 or £5 or even £50 per hour, depending on what they are doing. Then express the total volunteer input to your organisation each year as a cash sum. This can be included in a note to your accounts, but it can also be used in your publicity to show how you can add value to your work.

• Invest in your volunteers – their recruitment, their induction, their training, their supervision and their management. They an be a most valuable resource, particularly in hard times.

Who does the fundraising

One of the problems of fundraising is that few people actually enjoy doing it. Yet I suspect that people want to be asked to give, and want to give. Their generosity may be masked by our reluctance to ask them.

A typical answer to who actually does the fundraising may well be 'nobody'. Nobody is keen to do it. The job may be delegated to someone who is ill at ease doing it, and so doesn't do it. Or it may be deferred whilst other 'more priority' work is done.

This situation is obviously unsatisfactory. The following are a few suggestions to prevent this scenario from happening:

• The **trustees** (or the management committee) have the overall responsibility for seeing that the organisation has adequate resources to do an effective job, to support its current work programme and to help it develop for the future. Not every trustee may be interested in or good at fundraising, but collectively they must ensure that the fundraising strategies and efforts are sufficient for the task.

• Identify those **individual trustees** who have the skills, contacts and confidence to raise money successfully. Some organisations bring in people on to their board just for their fundraising capability. Others create development trusts or appeal committees where their particular talents will be specially useful. It is often worth conducting an 'audit' of the fundraising experience of your trustees and what contacts they have. You might be surprised.

• Allocate particular responsibilities to **staff**, which could include the director of the organisation, project leaders responsible for raising money for their projects or a fundraiser or fundraising team hired just for this purpose. The director or fundraising manager should assume overall responsibility for seeing that the work is done and for cultivating major relationships.

• Involve **volunteers**, who can add value to the fundraising effort. Some types of fundraising rely entirely on volunteers (such as street collections and many fundraising events). All organisations can use volunteers in some capacity to improve their fundraising.

• **Professional consultants** can and do raise money. But it will often be more cost effective and effective to do the fundraising yourself, relying on outside expertise to advise you, help draw up a strategy, develop a successful approach, produce effective materials or provide training.

The answer to the question 'Who does the fundraising?', is that somebody must. The strategy and direction must come from the top. Those doing it should have enough skills, commitment and tenacity to do a good job. They should be given sufficient time to plan and implement a fundraising programme, and they should be given the resources to be effective.

Fundraising provides the wherewithal for the organisation to succeed and to carry out its work. Insufficient priority, lack of leadership and direction from the top and the wrong people with inadequate resources can all lead to failure.

CHAPTER 8

RESERVES AND WORKING CAPITAL

BY KATE SAYER

What are reserves?

Reserves are the accumulated surpluses (or profits) which build up from day one in the life of an organisation. In a charitable context, they are unspent funds. They are not necessarily *cash* reserves, because the reserves may be invested in assets other than cash, such as buildings, equipment, stocks and shares.

The amount of your reserves can be calculated by adding the surpluses and subtracting the deficits incurred in each year to the present. This process is undertaken each year when the accounts are drawn up, so you can find out what your reserves are by looking at the balance sheet.

Sometimes the reserves are eroded because of losses and it is possible for an organisation to have negative reserves (accumulated losses or accumulated deficits). This means that more losses than profits have been made overall. The organisation can still survive in many cases, but it will need to get back to a position of having positive reserves to be viable.

Reserves are an estimate of the net worth of the organisation. This is a number on paper, but it should also represent real assets. Ultimately, if an organisation is wound up, the amount of the reserves would be a rough estimate of how much would be left over to be distributed. The actual amount would be affected by various commitments, contingencies and the real market value of the organisation's assets.

Different terminology is often used. Reserves may be called any of the following:

- Accumulated Surplus
- Accumulated Deficit
- General Fund
- General Reserve
- Retained Profits
- Accumulated Losses

In addition to the terms mentioned above, there may be specific reserves such as:

- Restricted Funds

EXAMPLE 1
Balance Sheet at 31 March

	£	£
FIXED ASSETS		
Land and Buildings		100,000
Furniture and Equipment		20,000
		120,000
CURRENT ASSETS		
Stock of Publications	3,000	
Debtors – unpaid sales invoices	1,000	
Cash at Bank	30,000	
	34,000	
CURRENT LIABILITIES		
Creditors-Unpaid purchase invoices	2,000	
PAYE and NI due	12,000	
Other Creditors and Accruals	5,000	
	19,000	
NET CURRENT ASSETS		**15,000**
NET ASSETS		**135,000**
RESERVES		**135,000**

In a Balance Sheet, the total reserves will equal the total net assets. This is inherent in the system of double entry accounting. For example, if we decided that the land and buildings of this organisation were only worth £80,000, then we would write their value down by £20,000, which would reduce the reserves by the same amount.

- Designated Funds
- Capital Reserve
- Earmarked Funds
- Committed Funds
- Endowment Funds

The terms 'funds' and 'reserves' are used interchangeably.

2. The need for reserves

Charities and voluntary organisations, in common with businesses, need reserves so that they have a 'buffer' or safety margin. This is really what is meant by *working capital*. In *Example 1*, the organisation has net current assets of £15,000. This represents the working capital of the organisation. It has sufficient money in the bank to pay off all the current liabilities, as well as having £11,000 left over to meet any other contingencies. This organisation is apparently in a healthy position... *apparently*, because we do not know what commitments or contingent liabilities exist. Such matters should be documented in the notes to the annual accounts.

Many organisations are far from being in this healthy position. Organisations which receive grant funding are usually required to spend all the grant by the end of the financial year, and to repay any amounts unspent.

Consequently, they have no balance of money left as reserves as the end of the year. Remember, reserves can only be built up if the organisation is making surpluses. If funders wish to ensure that their grant has been entirely spent for the purposes for which it was given, this does not allow the organisation to build up reserves.

Organisations taking on responsibilities for providing services need to ensure that they have sufficient working capital to run those services smoothly. They need a large enough buffer to be able to cope with delays in the receipt of income and to cover unexpected emergencies or unbudgeted expenditure. They should not be in a position where they lurch from crisis to crisis, with staff never being sure whether there is enough money left to pay them at the end of the year, or at the beginning of the new year when the grant for that year has yet to be confirmed.

Organisations without reserves are put in a position of extreme dependency for someone else's support before they can spend anything; dependency on everything going right; nothing to invest to help build a more secure future or to start up new areas of fundraising; nothing for emergencies. Good management and good financial planning are virtually impossible in a situation like this.

The position illustrated in *Example 2* demonstrates the difficulties experienced by grant funded groups. They are running a substantial operation. They are employing staff, and probably incurring liability in the event of any termination of their employment. Despite the fact that they have £30,000 in the bank, they have no reserves. No net worth at all. They may well be turned down for future funding on the basis of these accounts because they do not look viable!

EXAMPLE 2
Income and Expenditure Account for the year ended 31 March

	£	£
INCOME		
Grant Aid		350,000
EXPENDITURE		
Salaries	270,000	
Running Costs	80,000	
		350,000
SURPLUS		**Nil**

Balance Sheet at 31 March

FIXED ASSETS		Nil
CURRENT ASSETS		
Cash at Bank	30,000	
CURRENT LIABILITIES		
Creditors	30,000	
NET CURRENT ASSETS		**Nil**
NET ASSETS		**Nil**
RESERVES		**Nil**

This is an extreme example, and most organisations are better resourced than this. But very many do not have sufficient working capital or resources for their scale of operations, their responsibilities and their potential liabilities. Fortunately, many funders have begun to recognise the need for a healthy balance sheet and therefore allow organisations in receipt of grant funding to carry forward some surplus to the subsequent financial year.

Arguments for reserves

Whether you are accumulating surpluses from year to year, or if you are budgeting in your application for a sum to set aside as a reserve, you will need to be ready with some reasons for why reserves are needed. These are just some of the unforeseen expenditures which may arise:

- maternity leave cover
- long-term sickness of staff and related costs of providing cover
- building maintenance and redecoration (whether or not required under the terms of the lease or licence to occupy)
- recruitment costs
- complying with new laws (eg. health and safety and the VDU directive)
- replacement of equipment
- legal fees (eg. to contest an industrial tribunal).

Ways of dealing with some of these and presenting such issues in your accounts are dealt with in more detail in this chapter.

Development funds

You will also need reserves if you are to develop your organisation, as some investment may be needed. For example, you may decide that you have to become more self sufficient and less dependent on grants. You realise that to do so you need to build up a list of donors who will support your organisation. The investment in this plan has to be estimated to include the costs of the computer, software, training, data collection and entry onto the computer; the cost of producing the relevant publicity material, drawing up a membership scheme, and of setting up a covenant scheme; the cost of promotion to identify and recruit donors; and the cost of the expertise and the time to achieve all this. It will take time before any money is raised, and there will be a need to spend money first, which will eventually be recovered from the fundraising effort. The investment in this has to come either from grants and donations or from reserves you have built up.

Redundancy and winding up

Clearly if the organisation decides it no longer has a future, it will need sufficient reserves to pay out redundancy to all staff entitled to it. It will also need sufficient reserves to pay off any contracts or other liabilities. If there are insufficient reserves, then the trustees or management committee may be personally liable (if the organisation is unincorporated).

Provisions

Provisions are monies put aside from general reserves to cover future liabilities. Unlike a creditor, which is an actual liability of a known amount, the organisation will not have an unpaid purchase invoice for these future liabilities. The liability will certainly arise at some point in the future, but the timing and the exact amount are uncertain.

Situations where provisions are appropriate include liabilities arising under leases. A property lease may contain a clause which states that the tenant has to redecorate the outside of the building every five years. It would be appropriate to build up a provision for the redecoration costs. This is in accordance with the principal of 'matching' costs to the appropriate time period. The outside of the building will be weathering at an even rate over the five years, so the costs are being incurred evenly over that period. It is equitable and in accordance with the accruals concept to show some expense every year, rather than putting it all into year five.

In order to allocate sums as provisions, you must adopt a reasonable accounting policy and explain what that policy is in the notes to the

EXAMPLE 3
Provisions – accounting policy

Creative Arts Charity, a new organisation, has just taken a 25 lease on premises which it uses as an arts centre. No premium was paid to acquire the lease. A clause in the lease states that the premises have to be kept in good repair and that the outside should be redecorated every five years.

The trustees wish to ensure that the charity has sufficient funds to meet this obligation every five years, and so they decide to adopt the following accounting policy:

In accordance with the terms of the lease, the charity makes provision for the external redecoration of the premises used as an arts centre in such a way as to ensure that there are sufficient funds for the redecoration at the end of every five years.

In practical terms, the first step is to obtain an estimate of the cost of the redecorating works close to the first balance sheet date when the provision is to be made. Let's assume that the estimate is £15,000. The organisation has five years to save this sum, so in the first year they need to provide one fifth, being one year's worth of wear and tear.

At the end of the second year the cost of the redecorations should again be estimated at current prices. If inflation is 4%, this will amount to £15,600. Two years' provision will amount to two fifths of £15,600, which is £6,240. £3,000 has already been provided so a further £3,240 needs to be set aside for year two.

This procedure is continued until year five, when the redecorating works will be undertaken. The expenditure is shown as an expenditure with a transfer from the provision to cover four years' worth of work. If the final bill is higher than anticipated, then the extra cost has to be borne in the fifth year.

accounts. You must disclose the amounts being transferred to provisions in the year as well as the balances held as provisions in the balance sheet at the end of the year. You may not pretend that the money has been spent when it has not! Once you have developed an accounting policy for the particular area of expenditure, you should then apply it consistently from one year to the next.

Liabilities under leases are not the only situations where provision should be made. Other example include:

- replacement of equipment or vehicles
- contractual obligations under contracts of employment, such as sabbatical leave
- building additions such as fire escapes.

The terms of grants vary, so it may not be appropriate to make transfers to provisions from certain grants. Some funders prefer to receive a separate application for one-off spending (e.g. buying a new minibus) when the expenditure is to be incurred, rather than contribute each year to a provision.

Each situation should be considered on its merits, and advice can be sought from your auditors as to the most appropriate way to disclose such liabilities. Transfers to provisions are not the only option and may not be the appropriate procedure for all items.

Designated funds

This term can be used interchangeably with 'earmarked funds', and some organisations use the term 'committed funds' and mean the same thing. Funds may be designated at the discretion of the trustees for a particular purpose. This is not the same thing as *restricted funds* (which are explained further on).

When the charity receives donations or grants for its general charitable objects, the trustees may decide to allocate them to a particular project or activity. This is often the case when a charity receives a legacy or large one-off donation. This *designating of funds* makes it possible to separate out the unspent designated funds in the balance sheet. In this way, funds which have been earmarked for a particular purpose do not get absorbed into the general funds (reserves) of the organisation. They are kept separate, and used when required for the purpose for which they have been designated. At the same time the general (uncommitted) reserves are not inflated, because designated funds are excluded from this figure.

It is important to explain the purpose of the designated funds in a note to the accounts. Readers of your accounts should not be given the impression that you are trying to hide something. It is important also that the trustees make a proper decision to designate funds, which should be recorded in the minutes of trustees' meetings.

EXAMPLE 4
Designated Funds – accounting policy

Help the Homeless, a registered charity, received a legacy of £100,000 from a donor during the financial year. The trustees decided at a meeting that the funds should be placed in a special fund for the purchase of a new home for homeless people in Berkshire, where the donor had lived. Unfortunately, the amount would not be sufficient on its own and further funds would have to be raised before the project could commence. The funds were placed in a separate deposit account with high rates of interest, so that the fund could also accumulate the interest. The accounting policy adopted was:

The trustees designate funds to further particular purposes under the charitable objects when funds become available to the charity. The purpose of the funds so designated is to establish a new home for homeless people in Berkshire.

Designated Funds – accounting treatment
Income and Expenditure Account
for the year ended 31 March

	£
INCOME	
Grants, Donations, Charges etc.	500,000
Legacies	100,000
Total Income	**600,000**
EXPENDITURE	
Salaries and running costs	**470,000**
SURPLUS FOR THE YEAR	**130,000**
Added to Designated Funds	100,000
Appropriated to General Reserves	30,000

Balance Sheet at 31 March

		£
FIXED ASSETS		**750,000**
CURRENT ASSETS	300,000	
CURRENT LIABILITIES	150,000	
NET CURRENT ASSETS		**150,000**
NET ASSETS		**900,000**
RESERVES		
Designated Funds		100,000
General Reserves		800,000
		900,000

(The General Reserves for the previous year amounted to £770,000)

EXAMPLE 5
Restricted Funds – accounting policy

Charities need to state what the basis is for deciding whether funds are restricted or unrestricted. A third world charity might adopt the following policy:

Programme funds are restricted funds and are received from donors for onward transfer to projects in the countries where the charity operates.

Administration funds are unrestricted funds and are received from donors for the support costs such as salaries and running costs incurred in the course of administering the funds of the charity.

Restricted Funds – accounting treatment

Another year has passed for Help the Homeless charity. They still have the designated fund and in the year in addition to their other funding, they received specific funding of £300,000 for a three year programme.

Income and Expenditure Account for the year ended 31 March

	Restricted £	Unrestricted £
INCOME		
Grants and Donations	300,000	500,000
Interest	—	5,000
Total Income	300,000	505,000
EXPENDITURE		
Salaries and running costs	100,000	490,000
SURPLUS FOR THE YEAR	200,000	15,000

Balance Sheet at 31 March

	£	£
Fixed Assets		750,000
Current Assets	515,000	
Current Liabilities	150,000	
Net Current Assets		365,000
Net Assets		1,115,000
Restricted Funds		200,000
Unrestricted Funds		
Designated Funds		105,000
General Reserves		810,000
		1,115,000

Restricted funds

Charities often receive money from donors or grant funders where a restriction is imposed as to how the funds should be used. This is different from designated funds because it is not the trustees who make the decision about the restriction, the donors impose it. And this restriction is binding, unless the donor agrees to an alteration. With designated funds, the trustees can agree themselves to re-designate the funds or transfer them back to general funds. This is not possible with restricted funds. Frequently the conditions attached to a grant will be sufficient to make that funding restricted, although this will depend on the actual terms and conditions of the grant. If the funds, whatever the source, are restricted, then unspent balances at the end of the year have to be shown separately, and not absorbed into general funds. In addition, it is an accounting requirement to show separately the income and expenditure on restricted funds.

Endowment funds

Endowment has two meanings. Firstly, there is 'permanent endowment', which is money or assets given to the charity with the condition that it cannot be spent, but must be held for the charity's own use or to generate an income. This condition can only be removed with the consent of the Charity Commission. Endowment is also used more loosely to refer to money set aside as a capital reserve to generate a yearly income for the charity. Money can be set aside for this purpose by the trustees out of accumulated funds or on the request of a donor. Although the intention is to treat such a fund as capital, the trustees can decide to transfer sums from time to time to income and expenditure account to meet current expenditure requirements, if they so wish. Unlike for permanent endowment, there is no restriction on doing this.

Fixed assets

In the examples of the 'Help the Homeless' charity, it can be seen that it has substantial general reserves of approximately £800,000. It also owns fixed assets of approximately £750,000. This is not a coincidence! If a charity owns fixed assets, then these must have been funded in some way in the first place. In normal commercial accounting, it is quite normal for the business to make profits (which are added to reserves) and to plough these back into investments, such as new factories or equipment (fixed assets). A healthy business balance sheet has reserves so that it can make those investments.

Charities are different from commercial enterprises, however, and future fundraising may be jeopardised if funders perceive the charity as being too rich. Therefore, from this point of view, it may not be helpful to the charity to present the balance sheet as in examples 4 and 5. It may be wiser to identify the reserves which are funding the fixed assets. Many charities do this by 'labelling' some of the reserves as a capital fund. Example 6 shows how this might be done.

The charity should have a consistent accounting policy for dealing with fixed assets and capital funding. In many cases specific funding will have been received for significant assets, and this would be shown as a restricted fund.

EXAMPLE 6
Fixed Assets and Capital Fund
Balance Sheet at 31 March

	£	£
Fixed Assets		750,000
Current Assets	515,000	
Current Liabilities	150,000	
Net Current Assets		365,000
Net Assets		1,115,000
Restricted Funds		200,000
Unrestricted Funds		
Designated Funds		105,000
Capital Fund		750,000
General Reserves		60,000
		1,115,000

The solution is much more clearly stated in *Example 6,* that is:

- the charity has net current assets of £365,000
- this is not all 'free' money to spend as it wishes
- £105,000 of that amount has been designated for a new home in Berkshire
- £200,000 of that amount is funding for a specific project and can only be spent for that purpose (and would otherwise have to be given back to the donor)
- just £60,000 is in general reserves for working capital, contingencies and future expenditure.

The narrative report accompanying the annual accounts should explain the actual financial position. It will show that the charity is using its resources effectively and that it is not over-rich. It may be appropriate to make the point that the general reserves of £60,000 only represent about six weeks ordinary running costs. This is probably not as high as you would expect for a charity providing services.

Depreciation

Depreciation is a recognition of the wear and tear arising from the use of a fixed asset, and its corresponding loss of value. It is only an estimated amount, and the depreciation charged should be based on the estimated useful life of the asset. So buying a new minibus for a project, you make an estimate at the outset of how long you think the bus will last. Let's assume you buy the bus for £16,000 and you think it will last for four years. The simplest way to calculate the depreciation is to spread the cost equally over four years and make a depreciation charge in the income and expenditure of £4,000 in each of the four years. At the end of four years,

£16,000 will have passed through the income and expenditure account as the notional cost of wear and tear on the minibus. The asset will have nil 'book value', because according to the books the total amount originally spent on its purchase has been charged as a cost. The minibus may, in fact, still be running and continue in use for some years. If there is a significant difference between the original estimate of the life of the asset and its actual life, you might subsequently want to change the depreciation rate.

Depreciation represents the cost of using an asset during the period over which it is being used. Because the annual depreciation charge is an expenditure item, it reduces the surplus (or increases the deficit) that would otherwise have been shown. When the asset was first purchased, the purchase cost did not appear as an expenditure item, but was shown as a fixed asset on the balance sheet.

At the date of purchase, the organisation would have needed the cash resources to pay for the purchase. And this could only come out of reserves or through borrowing. The depreciation of the asset means that the organisation pays back the reserves of the initial cash outlay. It should not be confused with saving up to buy a replacement vehicle in the future.

Depreciation is spreading the cost of a vehicle which has already been bought; it does not mean that you have enough money to buy a new one. To do this, you would need to generate enough income to cover the depreciation charge *and* to build up a replacement provision as well. The provision would take account of inflation and the need to spend a larger sum on the replacement vehicle. The mechanism for making this provision has already been discussed.

The actual cost of using the asset is not just the running cost but must also include the depreciation and any replacement provision. If these are not taken into account in the annual budgeting and in grant applications relating to the project, the organisation will effectively be subsidising the service. It may decide to do this if it plans to replace the asset using grants raised specifically for this purpose. But this should be a conscious decision. If the organisation wants to generate the wherewithal to replace the asset by charging for its use, then it will need to recognise the true cost of using the asset and raise this sum from the grants and charges received for the project.

Stock

Stock is treated in much the same way as fixed assets. The cost of purchase is not charged to the income and expenditure account, and the value of the stock appears on the balance sheet as a current asset. The cost is shown as an expenditure as the stock is used up or if it is written down in value, in recognition that it is no longer commercially worth what it originally cost.

So as with the purchase of an asset, the organisation will need reserves to cover the purchase cost of the stock and to continue to hold the stock whilst it remains unsold.

What level of reserves?

The most difficult question to answer is what is an acceptable level of reserves for a charity.

Trustees have to balance a number of considerations:

On the one hand they want to provide sufficient resources to the organisation so that it can carry out its work effectively and pay for all the costs it is likely to incur. They may also want to give it a resistance and robustness that will allow it to weather periods of difficulty. If you have insufficient reserves, there is the danger that you will expose yourselves to insolvency if things go wrong. For example:

- a loss of a major grant;
- a change in the rules of a funding programme so that only certain costs now qualify
- a contract going wrong, where you are committed to providing a certain level of service whatever the cost of doing it
- an overspend or a major unbudgeted item of expenditure
- a trading loss, an event collapsing or a fundraising appeal failing to excite donors.

All these can create a financial crisis if you have nothing in reserve.

On the other hand, the trustees have a responsibility to act in the interests of the beneficiaries, which means that they should apply the money towards the need to the greatest extent they can, balancing this with the longer-term interests of sustaining a viable organisation. A further factor is that if the organisation appears 'too rich' (from a cursory examination of its accounts and balance sheet), this may make it more difficult to fundraise.

In determining an appropriate level of reserves, the following would serve to increase the amount of reserves you would need:

- **The cash position**: what working cash balances you need to cover current liabilities and to meet bills as they fall due.
- **Long-term commitments**: including leases, provisions under leases, contractual commitments you have entered into and any long-term responsibilities for your beneficiaries. This would include actual commitments for which you are legally liable and moral commitments.
- **Contingencies**: if a project had to close or if the organisation itself failed, what will the costs of closure be (redundancies, repayment of restricted funds, termination of leases and contracts). Or if at some time in the future, demand suddenly increased (for example through illness and famine) having money set aside would enable you to respond swiftly and effectively.
- **Capital and stock**: what are your current levels of assets and what growth will there be in the next few years. Any increase in your asset base has to be funded with a parallel increase in levels of reserves.

- **Risk**: are there particular areas of your work subject to risk? Obviously you will do all you can to manage the activity and manage the risk. But a cash reserve can protect you if things go wrong, and can 'buy you time' to retrieve the situation. This could vary from organisation to organisation – and will be anything from a postal strike to the failure of a fundraising campaign.

- **Growth**: if you are growing, will you need a consequent increase in working capital to finance this growth – to cover office space, equipment, increased activity and contingencies.

The following might be considerations for reducing the levels of working capital:

- **Flexibility** in your activity: can operations be curtailed, projects postponed, costs cut, if there is a reduction in income?

- **Donor goodwill**: do you have a large, active and enthusiastic band of supporters prepared to come to your aid in the event of need?

- **Access to borrowing**: can you borrow to tide you over a shortfall? Commercially or interest-free from supporters?

Every organisation is different, and the trustees or management committee members must develop their own policy on reserves based on their perception of the financial needs of the organisation, the demands on it to spend money now and the fundraising opportunities.

You may decide that you need a reserve of one month's expenditure. Or three months, or six months. Or one year. Or..... It is up to you to decide. But whatever you do decide, you must be able to justify as against spending the money now on the immediate needs.

Recently publicity has been given to charities which have very high levels of reserves; in one case, a charity allegedly had reserves equivalent to *six years* operating costs. The Charity Commission is considering issues around appropriate levels of reserves, but it must be remembered that what is considered appropriate for one type of charity may be completely inappropriate for another.

The benefits of having reserves

Reserves give you a greater flexibility to decide for yourself what you want to do and when you want to do it. They enable you to do things without always having to have 'permission' from a funder first.

Reserves allow you to invest now to generate income or save money in the future:

- to invest in fundraising
- to invest in income generation and
- to invest in the resources which will enable you to operate more efficiently and more effectively in the future.

Reserves give you time if things do go wrong. They are a buffer between misfortune and insolvency.

Reserves can give you greater self-confidence...

...but they can also create complacency and reduce the momentum and enthusiasm of the organisation. This is a danger to be aware of.

Accumulation for no purpose

Trustees should not accumulate funds for the sake of it! Indeed, this is poor stewardship if there are needs to be met. And if the charity can no longer fulfil its purposes, it should consider widening its objects or its beneficial area, and take advice from the Charity Commission. Collecting cash and investing it is not *per se* a charitable activity. Accumulating money for no purpose might jeopardise your charitable status. The Inland Revenue might feel that you are no longer operating for charitable purposes but using your tax-exempt status as a tax shelter. The Charity Commission might want to investigate on the basis that you are not fulfilling your trustee responsibilities.

It is, however, acceptable to establish a capital base, similar to an endowment fund, from which the charity can earn an income. The capital is left intact and only the income distributed. If you are intending to do this, your fundraising literature should clearly state the intention to set up a capital fund.

How to generate reserves

If you feel that your current level of reserves is insufficient, you might consider any or all of the following:

- **Have a policy on reserves**. As part of the strategic planning of your organisation and its finances, develop a policy on reserve levels. Decide what reserve level you feel is appropriate for your organisation, provide good reasons for this that will justify your decision to accumulate, and make the policy and the thinking behind it *explicit*, so that everyone (including your funders) knows precisely what you are doing and understand why you are doing it.

- **Set aside certain types of income**. Everything you raise each year has to be treated as income and appear as such in your accounts. But you may decide that certain categories of income can be set aside in your accounts and used to build your reserves. This could be legacy income. Or it might be the contribution of a friends' fundraising group (where they are happy to help you with your long-term fundraising).

- **A special appeal**. It may be your best bet to mount a special appeal, to bring together all your fundraising resources to raise a really large sum. This may be for a building, or it may be to create an endowment fund. If you are doing this, it is worth thinking about how to increase your appeal target to include the reserves you need. The appeal is a major fundraising opportunity, and if you miss it, you may no longer have the capacity to raise significant sums over and above your day-to-day needs.

How to present the reserves in the accounts

This is a critical issue, because if you get it wrong, you may find that you jeopardise your fundraising efforts. There are in fact two separate problems:

- The surpluses you show for each year, which you transfer to reserves;
- The balance sheet which may show large accumulated funds and cash balances.

The guiding principle in dealing with the situation is honesty. You know why you need to accumulate surpluses and build reserves; you can justify this as being appropriate and important to the financial future of the organisation; you have the job of explaining this to others. This can be done by putting notes to the accounts or through an openly stated policy that appears in your promotional literature.

Apart from this, there are mechanisms for adjusting the bottom line. For example, if you need to allocate money for particular purposes, you should create the appropriately designated funds. This will show in the balance sheet that the surplus funds are being accumulated for a particular purpose and the notes to the accounts will explain this. You can also on the income and expenditure accounts show the transfer as follows:

Total income for the year	700,000
Total expenditure for the year	620,000
Surplus for the year	80,000
Transfer to building development fund	70,000
Surplus to be carried forward	10,000

Working capital reserves

Precisely the same approach can be used if you are building up a working capital reserve, not for a particular project or purpose, but to underpin the organisation and meet its working capital requirements. To do this, a working capital reserve is created, transfers made to it each year, and an explanation given as a note to the accounts – explaining the need for working capital, the target level that the organisation intends to set aside, and the process for doing it, which might be by an allocation from the surplus or by setting aside particular categories of income such as legacies for this purpose.

CHAPTER 9

PROTECTIVE SOLUTIONS: LIMITING LIABILITY

BY MICHAEL NORTON

Some of the mechanisms for limiting liability have been covered earlier in the book in the context of limiting the exposure of trustees to personal liability *(see Chapter 5)*. Three strategies for doing this were suggested:

- Insurance against risk (also covered in the chapter) and trustee liability insurance to cover claims for breach of trust, negligence or wrongful trading, but not where guilty of a criminal act or where the trustee has acted deliberately or recklessly;

- Protecting trustee liability in contracts through inserting a clause to this effect on the contract;

- Incorporation of the charity to obtain protection for the trustees against the charity's losses, contractual breaches or other claims made against the charity. The most usual method of incorporation is to transfer the assets of the existing charity to a new charitable company with the consent of the Charity Commission.

This chapter explores possible mechanisms for reducing your organisation's exposure to liability and for protecting your organisation against loss or failure. Four themes are discussed:

- Organisational structures for protecting and managing the different assets and activities you are responsible for;

- Assessment of risk and insurance against it;

- Assessing exposure to liability, and developing management and financial strategies to cover this (see Chapters 7 and 8);

- Protecting your organisation's interests when entering into contracts.

Organisational structures

Most charities and voluntary organisations have quite simple organisational structures. A single organisation, perhaps with a commercial trading subsidiary attached to it (which is required to preserve the organisation's charitable status and to obtain tax relief on the trading profits). And perhaps also with a network of local branches or independently constituted and run affiliated groups.

But there is the possibility of more complex structures, and there are some good strategic and management reasons for having these. Perhaps the charity of tomorrow will be a much more complex animal than the charity of today. Here are some of the possibilities to consider:

- **Independent charities to undertake contract work** (or trading subsidiaries for this purpose if the contract work is not charitable). This creates an *arms length relationship* between the parent charity and the contracting organisation. It creates a *legal barrier* between the assets of the parent charity which may have been built up over many years and the contract activity. In the event of failure to deliver the contract, the parent charity and its assets are protected. Any premises or management services provided by the parent charity can be charged out at a reasonable rate – so that the contract is not inadvertently being subsidised. Other transfers between the two organisations could be paid as grants (where both organisations exist for similar charitable purposes).

- **Property trusts**, to hold the charity's property separate from its operations. In the event of failure, the property is still held on charitable trusts and available for public benefit. The user of the property would of course contribute towards its maintenance and upkeep.

- **Development and fundraising trusts**, to raise money for development. This is kept separate from the charity's funds, but paid over for certain specified (restricted) purposes. This arrangement has the benefit that the fundraising for future development can be managed separately by people whose particular skills lie in doing this, that attention is paid to the organisation's future, and that the terms under which any grants are made to the parent charity are such that they preclude any possibility of clawback. The trustees of the development trust have their interests aligned with the donors, to ensure that the money they raise is spent effectively for the organisation's development.

- **Fundraising groups and friends' organisations**. The 1992 Charities Act imposes some restrictions on the ways in which money is raised and accounted for, and it puts burdens on the trustees of the charity to see that everything is done properly. It also provides a remedy for unauthorised fundraising, where the trustees believe that this is not in the best interests of the charity – through a request to desist, followed if necessary by an injunction. Fundraising by local branches or support groups can cause problems, as the fundraising is being undertaken in the name of the charity often with insufficient control being exercised by the trustees. An alternative is to constitute the fundraising groups as independent organisations with the purpose of raising money for the parent charity. They will then be governed and managed by their own trustees. The parent charity might then require a legal agreement for the use of its name, logo and connection and require an approved constitution to be adopted and certain performance standards met. This is a concept of a 'franchised' fundraising organisation.

- **Endowment trusts** to hold and manage the charity's endowments, separately from its other assets.

- **Project trusts** for separating out major projects into separate operating charities, again so that the appropriate management skills and resources can be developed for each. This might be done on a 'divisional' basis according to the type of work, or on a 'regional' basis.

The disadvantages of any complicated structure are:

- The additional legal, accounting and administrative costs that will be incurred;

- Difficulties in funding the original charity, if lucrative projects are 'hived off';

- Possible difficulties in transferring funds from one organisation to another, or in using funds from one area of work to cross-subsidise another, underfunded, area of work;

- The necessity of ensuring adequate communication and co-operation between the different organisations;

- Difficulties in future if the organisations develop differently, or have different priorities – for example if the trustees of a property trust want to use part of the building for work with local children, but the management committee of the original charity want to use it for work with elderly people;

- Difficulties in future if subsidiary, divisional or regional charities become larger than the original charity.

The advantages of separation are:

- Focused management appropriate to the particular activity of each unit;

- A protection against failure;

- Transparency in costs and subsidies and informed decisions in calculating these;

- More control over how the organisation's resources and needs are presented, which may assist fundraising or prevent clawback.

The advantages and disadvantages of a more complex structure should be carefully weighed up before any decision to fragment the organisation is taken.

Insuring against risk

There are two ways of insuring against risk – changing what you do or how you do it to lessen or avoid the risk altogether, or taking out an insurance policy to cover you in the event of loss.

There are a wide range of insurances that most organisations have to protect themselves and the trustees against loss. Some are mandatory, most are entered into freely. They include:

- employer's liability insurance
- redundancy insurance
- public liability insurance
- fidelity insurance and money insurance
- professional indemnity insurance
- defamation insurance
- product liability insurance
- personal accident insurance
- building insurance
- insurance of building contents, equipment and other property
- vehicle insurance
- trustee liability insurance
- insurance of particular events (a fundraising event against rain, for example).

Trustees need to do an analysis of the risks the charity is running and look particularly at the following:

- **For insured risks**

   What is covered; what is excluded?

   In what circumstances can claims be made; and in what circumstances will claims be refused?

   How much is insured; and how does this relate to the loss sustained or the cost of replacement?

   How much does this cost, and does this represent good value for money in relation to the risk?

- **For uninsured risks**

   What is the nature of the risk, its size (worst case) and the probability of this occurring?

   Are the consequences of the potential risk too high a burden (especially where there is a very small chance of it occurring) which warrants an insurance?

   How much will the insurance cost, and is it worth paying?

- **For all risks**

   What management action can be undertaken to reduce the risk or the chance of it happening?

   What costs can be underwritten at the outset to avoid or reduce the risk?

Assessing liability

Liabilities fall into several different categories:

- actual liabilities
- looming liabilities
- potential liabilities
- potential losses
- contingent liabilities.

All these affect the financial health of the organisation

- **Actual liabilities** include all debts incurred by the organisation which are due or which will fall due at some time in the future. You need to know what these are and when they are due for payment. You need to have the resources to meet them or to be making provisions towards them.

- **Looming liabilities** include all those known expenditures which are impending, but where no liability has yet been incurred, particularly special or major items of expenditure. Such things as a development plan scheduled to start soon would be included. These are not actual liabilities, in that a decision could be taken if necessary to cancel the expenditure. But they are plans against which resources have to be obtained.

- **Potential liabilities** are those items where the organisation would become liable if something were to go wrong. It is these items that are most often covered by insurance. There is no indication that they will go wrong, but if they do they could cause considerable loss. Theft, damage, injury, negligence... It is one of the jobs of the Trustees to ask 'What if...?' and to explore whether there are any potential liabilities facing the organisation which could cause severe problems. And if so, what should be done about this.

- **Potential losses**, where an organisation is trading, the possibility of making a loss always exists. Trading, earning money through fees and charges and ancillary income generation schemes are all becoming increasingly important to charities, and this requires managerial, entrepreneurial and marketing skills as much as the traditional skills needed to fund and run an organisation. It may also require a certain level of working capital to underpin it.

- **Contingent liabilities** are those liabilities which are contingent on some other occurrence such as the withdrawal of a grant, a default on a contract or the closing down of an activity or of the organisation itself. Unexpended grants for restricted purposes, money received in advance for goods or services not delivered, contractual obligations of the delivery of a service, liabilities to employees and possibly to beneficiaries, liabilities stemming from leases or rental arrangements for property and equipment: all these would be paid out of future income in the normal course of events, but would become an immediate liability if operations were to cease today. Equally a default on a contract could lead to the contract being terminated and claims being made against the organisation for recompense. Or if the organisation is dependent on the skills of a particular member of staff and that person for whatever reason leaves or becomes unavailable for work, then this could have serious financial consequences. All these contingent liabilities need to be borne in mind, particularly if the organisation is in a position of financial weakness or a major grant seems insecure.

Trustees (and financial managers) should:

- Try to assess the nature and extent of all these liabilities
- Consider the implications for the organisation and its future, and also in relation to their own personal liability. It may be that the extent of the organisation's liabilities requires more fundraising, more working capital and a stronger reserves base.

Protecting your organisation's interests on contracts

One particularly important area of liability is that stemming from contracts. These include leases, maintenance or rental agreements for equipment and contractual arrangements for the delivery of services. Whether you contract to provide a service, or to receive a service, the principles are the same.

The point of a contract is to define the arrangement and protect both or all parties if things go wrong. Unfulfilled obligations or termination penalties or guarantees can all cause problems. The following is a checklist for avoiding liability (or at least being aware of the liabilities you are exposing yourselves to) when entering into the contract.

- Read and understand the contract. Know what you are expected to do, how performance failure will be assessed and what happens if you fail to deliver what you have contracted to do. Know what the implications of all this are for the organisation and also for you personally as trustee.
- Take legal advice from your professional advisers.
- Where trustees would be personally liable in the event of failure, try to get this liability specifically written out of the contract, such that any liability is then restricted to the assets of the organisation. This would put charity trustees on a par with company directors, who incur no personal liability from the contracts that the company enters into.
- Avoid agreeing to find guarantors. Your failure puts them at risk.
- Negotiate effectively to get the contract you want for the services that you are confident you can deliver.

- Try not to have termination penalties included in the contract in the event of early termination by you. These will be paid out of your charitable funds and reduce the amount you have available to meet the need.
- Have the length of the contract suit your requirements, with options to terminate early or to extend to suit you.
- Have any notice on their part to be given of early termination of a sufficient length for you to able to make alternative arrangements -for the beneficiaries, for the staff, for the use of the premises as appropriate.
- Match the obligations you enter into in dealing with subcontractors, employees, etc. to the terms of the contract. So any termination of the contract does not leave you with obligations you cannot fulfil or have not provided for.
- Include in the costings sufficient to cover **all** costs, to make all relevant provisions, to cover contingencies and even to leave an element of profit at the end. Remember a contract is not a grant. You don't (or shouldn't) have to justify it in terms of the costings, but in terms of the nature and quality of the service you contract to deliver. Good negotiating sills can lead to better contracts.

APPENDIX 1

AN AGENDA FOR FUNDERS

AN AGENDA FOR FUNDERS

Some charities do have enormous reserves, particularly those well endowed with land or investments or via a major public appeal. Many large charities maintain an adequate reserve level, balancing the need to spend with the need to survive. But many charities do not, and this includes a large number which are primarily funded by one or several large grants from statutory sources and which have not been able to create their own independent sources of income. Such organisations are at the mercy of their major donors. The problem of too low reserves is a shared problem stemming equally from the approach of funders to funding, and the response of grant-seekers in an extremely competitive environment:

- **A hand to mouth approach**. Many grant-seekers only raise money when they need it. All money is related to a particular year's expenditure, or to particular projects.

- **Underfunding**. Because fundraising is hard and because applicants pare their budgets to an absolute minimum, applications are pared to an absolute minimum. At the same time, donors may be part-funding a project, challenging the applicant to raise the balance elsewhere. And some donors refuse to cover the costs of depreciation, provisions, contingencies.

- **Pressure from funder**. Most funders do not like to see accumulated reserves. They take the view that if the charity if *not* spending what it has, then it has no right to ask for more. Their first scrutiny is of the accounts. If there are large surpluses at the end of the year, or large amounts held as cash balances, this would be a justification for their not making a grant.

- **Clawback**. More pernicious still is the practice of clawback. It is obviously correct that if the money is not spent and cannot be spent for the purposes for which it was given, then it should be repaid. But even here a lenient view might be taken if the recipient can come up with an alternative purpose for the money acceptable to the donor. Some funders go further, and clawback any additional funds that a charity succeeds in raising. This is an effective brake on a charity doing anything to sort itself out financially. It also means that the grant-maker will be left funding all those that can't or won't fund themselves – penalising success and rewarding failure or inertia.

If the problems are in part due to the actions of funders, the solutions also lie in part with the funders, who have the means to encourage their applicant clients to become financially stronger. The following are some things that funders might do:

- **Recognise the need for reserves**. A recognition that successful organisations need a reasonable level of operating reserves is a first step. Waiting on penury as a prerequisite for applicants will only lead to an under-resourced voluntary sector unable to do its job.

- **Encourage properly costed applications**. This may mean making known to applicants that they should include all the costs in the budget. It will mean allowing depreciation and provisions as cost items. It may mean suggesting to applicants that they may have undercosted their proposal, and asking them to revise their budget and submit a larger application.

- **Develop partnerships**. The applicant and the funder work together to achieve a charitable aim. The applicant does the work, the funder provides the money. This concept of partnership can be carried through to the funding relationship, where the funder provides a reasonable grant over a reasonable period of time and help or advice in raising the balance of the funding, if this is needed. At the same time the funder should insist that there be ideas for how the project will be eventually funded after the initial phase, and even provide money in the budget to help the project move on.

- **Explore investment possibilities**. There are many possibilities for 'investing' in an organisation, for providing money and to help save money or generate income in the future. Investment in research, in development, in marketing, in fundraising, in efficiency, in facilities can help achieve this. Spending money this way may not help need in the short term, but it may help the recipient operate much more effectively in the future. At a time when demand for available funds continues to increase, it may make sense to help organisations to become more effective, than just tide them over for another year. This is an investment approach to grant-making, rather than providing support or a subsidy for the service.

- **Drop the practice of clawback**. Or rather, encourage the development of fundraising and the development of a greater degree of financial independence and viability amongst those organisations that are supported.

If lack of reserves is a financial problem, then those responsible for funding the voluntary sector have an important role to play. Taking a strategic role as a stakeholder, they are in a position to help create strong and sustainable organisations.

APPENDIX 2

CHECKLIST

CHECKLIST

The following are some of the more usual points which can lead to financial problems. You should check and assure yourself that everything is alright.

1. Income tax, National Insurance, PAYE

- All amounts due to the Inland Revenue should be paid on the due date. These can be large amounts, and getting into arrears is often the start of rapid financial decline.

- Ensure that all payments for casual work and all payments to people who say they are self-employed meet the requirements of the Inland Revenue. If Income Tax and National Insurance are not deducted when they should be, the amounts you have paid out can be treated as net payments (after deduction of basic rate tax and National Insurance), and the amount due to the Inland Revenue can be nearly as much again. Check that you are making deductions as required and setting aside sufficient to cover potential liabilities to the Inland Revenue.

2. VAT

If you are registered for VAT:

- All amounts due should be paid on the due date (as for Income Tax). Any VAT you charge is collected by you on behalf of Customs and Excise and must be handed over.

- Ensure that VAT is being charged on all taxable supplies that you are making, and that the tax is accounted for properly in your books.

- Ensure that the required documentation is kept on file to substantiate any recovery of Input Tax.

- Take professional advice or consult Customs and Excise or get a ruling from the VAT Administration Directorate on all grey areas. You may find that what you consider to be a donation or a grant is in practice considered a taxable supply and subject to VAT. Keep a particular eye on membership income, sponsorship payments (where the return to the company is more than a simple acknowledgement), income received on services supplied under a contract, and income from exempt training.

- Where you make exempt and taxable supplies and are benefiting from the *de minimis* partial exemption rules for reclaiming Input Tax, keep an eye on your turnover and its composition to ensure that you continue to comply with the conditions for reclaiming all the Input Tax.

Where you are near the VAT registration threshold:

- Keep an eye on how your turnover is developing, and take professional advice on registration as appropriate.

3. General solvency of the organisation

- Ensure that the financial controls are adequate in relation to the complexity of the organisation, and that the possibilities of loss as a result of error or fraud are minimised.

- Assure yourselves that the organisation has sufficient cash resources to meet its immediate liabilities and to continue to do so for the foreseeable future (the Cash Flow Test).

- Assure yourselves that the organisation has sufficient assets to cover its liabilities, and that this position will continue for the foreseeable future (the Balance Sheet Test). Assure yourselves that the assets are being valued on a realistic basis (particularly if there has been a recent downturn in the market).

- Where either the organisation's current assets or its net worth give cause for concern, particular care should be taken. Finance staff and trustees should keep a close eye on the situation; meet regularly to monitor progress; take professional advice where appropriate; minute their decisions; formulate a turnaround strategy; and implement it.

4. Deposits and investments

- Make sure that your cash balances are deposited with financially secure institutions.

- Where you are obtaining a seemingly very high rate of return from your deposits (particularly where the money is deposited with smaller institutions), take professional advice. If there seems to be any cause for caution, limit the amounts you deposit with any one institution to spread the risk. The financial failure of someone else can trigger your own.

- Take seriously your trustee investment responsibilities: diversify your investments to avoid risk; take advice in writing as you are required to do under trust law and charity law; review your investments and investment returns and performance regularly (at least annually, and for larger organisations, quarterly).

5. Restricted funds

- Ensure that all restricted funds are kept separate in your accounts, and that they are not being used for purposes other than for which they were given.

- Ensure that all grant income is being spent for the purposes for which it was given and that all conditions of grant are being met.

- Ensure that your fundraising approach is not restricting the purposes for which you are receiving the money without your being aware of this.

6. Contracts for providing services

- Ensure that you are fulfilling your contract obligations (to the letter). Understand the consequences for not doing so – including claims for redress that may be made against you and penalty clauses.

- If you are taking over the running of a service from another body, go through the contract in detail to determine your obligations and liabilities, and also investigate whether and to what extent you are subject to the provisions for the transfer of undertakings in respect of any liabilities to employees. If you are, then you will need to provide for the liabilities you have taken on.

7. Leases and other contractual obligations

- Be aware of any obligations under any lease rental agreement or other contract you have entered into (such as photocopier rental agreements), and that you are making sufficient provision or have adequate reserves to meet the obligations when they fall due. One particular problem can be the dilapidation clauses in property leases. Read the small print!

- If you are near the limits of solvency and are unincorporated, be aware of the personal liabilities which might arise under any contracts or leases if you cease to operate.

- Check who actually is responsible for the lease. Check for any guarantees against default which may have been included in the agreement.

- If you have assigned a lease which is still current, remember that you can still be held responsible in the event that the assignee defaults. Check that the assignee is continuing in operation and is in a position to continue to meet the obligations under the lease.

8. Insurance

- Check that you have current insurance policies to cover all matters where insurance is statutorily required.

- Check that you are insured against public liability and have professional indemnity insurance (if this is appropriate).

- Check that any essential property and assets used in the course of your work are properly insured, and that in the event of loss your insurance claim plus any provisions you have set aside will be sufficient to cover the liability.

9. Stock and current assets

- Ensure that stock is valued realistically, and that its value is being written down or written off if unsaleable.

- Ensure that there is a realistic chance of recovering any amounts due to you in full. Ensure that people who owe money to you are being chased up quickly and effectively as soon as their payments fall due, and see that bad debts are written off.

10. Local branches

- If you operate through local branches or have associated groups (either to fundraise or to deliver services), check the status of these (whether they are autonomous or an integral part of your organisation), then ensure that they are not creating any liabilities for which you will be held responsible.

- In the light of the Charities Act 1993, you may wish to review the legal structure of your organisation, its branches and affiliates.

11. Forward planning and funding

- The best way to avoid insolvency is to manage your affairs properly and to plan well ahead. Ensure that you are thinking strategically, looking forward, taking into account future obligations, planning your fundraising to match your needs, and managing the fundraising effectively to ensure that it produces what you need.

- Assess the long-term status of your major funding sources. Make every attempt to get these put on to a secure basis, and to see that you receive adequate notice of any cut or termination, such that you can take remedial action.

- Try to get provision for winding down costs written into conditions of grant aid for the larger grants you receive. Some local authorities, for example, will provide three months' running costs when they terminate a grant.

- Diversify your funding base to minimise the risk of failure arising from the termination of any one grant or the loss of any particular source of income.

- Manage your income generation activities in a business-like way – including income generation by an associated trading company, whose failure may affect your own financial health.

- If there is a need for working capital, discuss and decide a policy on this, and build this into your financial and fundraising strategy.

- Consider a large capital appeal as a method of securing your organisation's future (at least in the medium term). Note any anniversaries or other events which this might be tied to. If you decide to proceed, do this professionally and give yourself the time to succeed.

12. Your legal status and organisational structure

- Check that your organisation's legal status is appropriate for its current scale of activity and obligations, and that it does not put the trustees unduly at risk.

- Check that your constitution is clear and workable, and verify that it gives the trustees sufficient powers to retain control at a time of difficulty. If you are unhappy with the constitution, consider taking steps to amend and modernise it to meet your current and future needs.
- As trustees, understand how insolvency might affect you, and consider changing the legal structure if you feel unhappy with what you have at present.

INDEX

INDEX